The Best
FREE
THINGS
in America

Linda & Bob Kalian

Library of Congress Cataloging-in-Publication Data
Kalian, Robert
Kalian, Linda

The Best Free Things In America

ISBN 0-934968-20-9

1. Consumer Reference   2. Catalog Free Things

Quantity discounts are available. Teachers, fund raisers, premium users, contact us at the address below regarding the quantities needed.

Publisher: Roblin Press, 388 Tarrytown Road - Upper Level, White Plains, NY 10607
(914) 220-6509   Fax: (914) 220-6501

Be sure to visit our Web site at: **www.freethingsusa.com**

CONTENTS

A Few Words Before We Start

You're about to embark on a fascinating journey, the journey to the world of *Free Things*. Most people have no idea just how many fantastic things are waiting for them free for the asking. Before you begin, read the few tips we've included below.

1. Save money - use a postcard whenever possible (unless they request a SASE or a nominal shipping charge – (there aren't many of these).

2. SASE — means send a long (#10) self-addressed stamped envelope. Your freebee will be returned to you in your own envelope.

3. Be sure to include your ZIP CODE - Without it you may never receive your gift (since many items are sent to you via third class mail).

4. Ask for the items you want by name. Often companies will have several gifts available and won't know which one you're asking for unless you specify.

5. Teachers, civic and religious groups: If you'd like quantities of any item, ask for it and mention what it's for. Usually you'll get the quantity you need.

6. If you use a product or have any favorable comment to make, the companies appreciate hearing about it. Many of these freebies are part of a company's efforts to get you to know...and hopefully like...their products. They appreciate a kind word (don't we all.)

7. Be patient. Some gifts may start coming within a week or two but others take longer - often a month or even more. The reason is that companies are often flooded with requests and it takes time to process them.

8. We have added a lot of internet addresses wherever possible. Be sure to visit these web sites where you will find a ton of great information (and often even free samples, books and lots more). If you don't yet have your own computer, visit your local library where they are sure to have a computer you can use.

9. Every item was available at the time the book was written. However, sometimes supplies of an item may run out and the offer may be withdrawn or replaced with a new freebie. (Please let us know at the addess below if you come across any of these so we can update the next edition of this book...thanks). Also, if you come across a freebie that you particularly like and would like to share with others, please write to us and tell us about it. If we use it in our next edition, you will receive a copy of that book... free of course... as our thanks.

10. Have Fun!

Roblin Press
Dept BFT-204
PO Box 125
Hartsdale, NY 10530

DEDICATION

To our son Dennis who has courageously
faced the most difficult challenge of his
young life in his battle with lymphoma.

We always knew you were strong
But never this strong!
"Word to the strength!!"

Something For Everyone

Free For The Asking – Right In Your Back Yard

The first thing to remember is that there are lots of things all around you that are free for the asking. All you have to do is be aware of them and to *ASK*. Let's take a look at a few examples:

FREE FOR CONSUMERS

Supermarket bulletin boards offer free items that neighbors may want to get rid of or trade.

Credit card companies offer free month trials on discount shopping clubs, travel, insurance and offer all kinds of specials. The one thing you have to remember is if you don't want it, after the month is up, cancel it.

You can even get free magazine subscriptions, tapes and CD's just for asking. Always remember to look in your local paper for deals at the supermarkets for buy one item, get one free.

FREE TICKETS

If you enjoy watching TV shows, you'll enjoy it that much more when you're watching it live right at the TV studio. Now there's an easy online way to get free TV tickets for yourself and your guests to almost any show that has a live audience. On your computer (if you don't have a computer, use the one at your local library) log onto this web site and you will not only get instant tickets to your favorite TV show for up to 6 people but you'll also get a detailed map to the TV studio – all printed out on your printer. Visit their web site at:
www.tvtix.com

FREE TICKETS TO TV SHOWS

The TV networks will provide you with free tickets to any of their shows that have audiences. If you plan to be in Los Angeles or New York and would like to see a TV show write to the network (care of their 'Ticket Department') before your visit. Generally you will get a letter you can exchange for tickets for any show open at the time of your visit. Write to:

ABC, 320 West 66 St. New York, NY 10023. In Los Angeles: Call 818-753-3470 Ext. 214. Paramount Guest Relations 323-956-1777, or on the web: www.paramount.com Then Click on "studio."

CBS Ticket Div., Television City 7800 Beverly Blvd., Los Angeles, CA 90036. In New York, 524 W. 57 St., New York, NY 10019

NBC, 3000 West Alameda Ave.. Burbank, CA 91523 (or 30 Rockefeller Plaza, New York, NY 10112) Or go to their web site at: www.nbc/footer/ NBC_Studio_Pass.shtml

Oprah, In Chicago: call 312-575-2458 or visit them on the web at: www.oprah.com
Check out these useful websites:
www.abc.com
www.nbci.com
   www.nytix.com

SWEET SCENTS

Now you can freshen your home with a beautiful lace sachet filled with sweet smelling potpourri. Use it in a drawer to freshen lingerie or even in a closet to refresh your linens. It makes a great gift. Send six first class stamps postage and ask for a *Scented Sachet.* Send to:
Sweet Scents
2431 Buck Rd.
Harrison, MI 48625

FREE PETS

There's really no reason to spend hundreds of dollars for a pet. Check your local paper. They often have ads for free kittens and pups when their pets have litters. Animal shelters also have some of the cutest puppies & kittens just dying for a home. The pets are free...most often they will only ask you to pay for the shots.

FREE LAND FILL/FIRE WOOD

Some contractors offer free land fill and free top soil when they want to get rid of it. The only catch might be that you have to remove it (or pay a nominal delivery charge.) Check out construction sites. You can often get free fire wood when they are clearing the land.

FREE COMPUTER SERVICES

There are tons of offers to try different things before you buy. For example computer online services offer a variety of *free trials* just to get you to try their service and to surf the Internet. Call:
AMERICA ON LINE (CURRENTLY OFFERING 700 FREE HOURS JUST FOR SIGNING ON): 1-888-265-8002
PRODIGY: 1-800-776-3449
COMPUSERVE: 1-800-848-8990

LOOKING GOOD

Free haircuts are available through some of your local beauty and barber schools. Check your phone book and give them a call. Some may ask a small fee or a tip for the trainee. Some of your larger hair designers may offer free style and cuts certain months or certain times of the year. Call your favorite salon and find out when they are training their students. You benefit by getting the designer him/herself for free. (In their salon they may charge anywhere from $50.00 and up.) Companies like Clairol often offer free hair coloring when they are testing new products. Don't hesitate to give any of them a call. Remember, if you don't ask you'll never know.

Want to try free perfume or have a makeover? Try any one of your larger department stores. You are never obligated to buy and some of the companies will even give you free product samples. You could have a ball going from store to store. Next time you need a new look, try your local department store.

FREE TRAVEL

There are lots of options around for free or almost free travel. The airlines offer you free tickets for changing your flight if they are overbooked. So next time you are at the airport ready to take a flight, volunteer to be 'bumped'. Typically you'll be put on a flight leaving an hour or so later and get a free ticket for a future flight.

Also, frequent flyer plans are still a good deal. Make sure you are a member of the airline's frequent flyer club if you plan on doing any airline travel. When you build up enough travel miles you will qualify for free airline travel.

If you have a unique specialty, many cruise lines will give you a free trip when you give a lecture about your specialty on one of their cruises. They often have theme cruises you might fit in with. For example, if you are a fitness specialist they often look for people to teach aerobics on board. So if you have a special skill, the cruise line might feel it is special enough to give you a free trip if you spend a few hours instructing others while on the cruise. Check the toll-free directory for the phone numbers of the cruise lines.

There are some courier services that will ask you to carry a package anywhere in the world they travel to. With that you get a free trip for carrying the parcel. Sometimes you can get to stay a few extra days as long as you can catch their plane on the return flight.

When they travel, some families look for housesitters. In return for watching their home, you get a free place to live. If you like to travel, you can might even trade apartments and homes with people in other parts of the country (or the world) through different real estate exchanges. Check the classified section of your local newspaper.

FREE FOR USING YOUR CREDIT CARD

The credit card war is heating up...and you stand to benefit. Today more and more banks and companies are offering credit cards that come with added bonuses for using it. For example, some banks offer credit cards that give you one frequent flyer mile for each dollar you charge on their card. You can use the miles to get free airline tickets. Also, many larger chain stores offer you free dollars to spend in their store just for opening a charge account with them. There is no obligation to use the card and you can cut it up if you don't plan to use it.

FREE ENTERTAINMENT

Don't overlook all the free concerts and theatre productions in all community parks outdoors especially in the summer months. Check with your local parks and recreation department.

Many local movie theatres have deals on slow nights. Our local movie theatre offers a special on Tuesday nights: Buy one ticket, get one free. Check it out in your area.
If you like concerts and drama some theatre and opera companies offer ushers (if you are willing to work a shift) free tickets in exchange for your work.

These are just a small handful of the tons of free and practically free offers all around you all the time. The important thing is to keep an eye out for them and take advantage of them where they are of interest to you.

FREE DINNER

Don't forget that there are many restaurant chains that offer you a free dinner on your birthday. All you have to show is a license or some proof of your birthdate.

Also check the ads for local restaurants that offer those great coupons for buy-one dinner get-one free.

FREE LONG DISTANCE CALLS

Because of all the competition between phone companies, if you are willing to switch they'll offer you all kinds of deals from $100.00 checks to several hours of free calls. Shop around for the best deal before you sign up with another phone company. First, take advantage of the free offers. Don't be hesitant about switching phone companies...you can always switch again to another company that offers you an even better deal.

ELDERCARE BY PHONE

Getting help and information about services for older people anywhere in the United States is now possible. There is a new national *Eldercare Locator* service. Dial: **1-800-677-1116** between 9 a.m. and 5p.m. Monday through Friday. Have the name and address of the person to be assisted, the zip code and a brief description of the service or information needed. The "Eldercare Locator" provides information about adult day -care centers, legal assistance, home health services and more. This service taps into a nationwide network of organizations familiar with state and local community services throughout the country.

If you would like you can also check out the Eldercare Locator on the Internet at: **www.aoa.dhhs.gov**

BOOK BARGAINS

Catalog of Book Bargains is for all book lovers that want to save 90% or more off original prices. Some recent best sellers are included in this 50 page catalog. Free from:

P. DAEDALUS BOOKS INC.
BOX 9645 GERWIG LANE
COLUMBIA, MD 20146
OR CALL: **1-800-395-2665**
Or visit them on the web at:
www.salebooks.com

PROBLEM TEENS

If you are having a lot of trouble dealing with your teen age child, there's a toll free phone number you can call for help. To help you deal with the problem constructively Covenant House offers you tips that have been proven to work. These helpful tips will open lines of communication and help keep you in touch with your child before he/she gets out of hand. If you need expert advice or support, call their NINELINE at **1-800-999-9999**. They will put you in touch with people who can help you right in your own town.

RAISING YOUR GRANDKIDS

If you are in the position of raising your grandchilden, you will want to get this free newsletter. Called *Parenting Grandchildren, A Voice For Grandparents* it is chuck full of useful information. Write to:

AARP GRANDPARENT INFO CENTER
601 EAST STREET NW
WASHINGTON, DC 20049
www.igrandparents.com

FRESH BREATH

These great *Fresh Breath Capsules* will help you cure your bad breath internally. Dont worry...the next time you eat garlic or spicy food, pop one of these Breath Fresh capsules. They also have other great products like Retinol A, Ultramins plus Vitamins and Thigh Cream. To try the Breath Freshener, send $1.00 to cover postage and handling to:

21ST CENTURY GROUP
10 CHESTNUT STREET
SPRING VALLEY, NY 10877

"THE GOOD LIFE CATALOG"

If you are a cigar smoker or know someone who is, this catalog is a must. Not only will you find every cigar you can think of, but all the accessories that go with them. There is a Cigar Hall of Fame and even some unusual and interesting gifts for people who don't smoke. Drop a card to:

THE THOMPSON COMPANY
5401 HANGAR COURT
P.O. BOX 30303
TAMPA, FL 33630-3303
800-216-7107
OR VISIT THEIR WEB SITE AT: WWW.THOMPSONCIGAR.COM

BEST FOOT FORWARD

When your feet ache and you are looking for some kind of relief what can you do? The Podiatric Association of America has a toll-free number you can call to get assistance. Call:

1-800-FOOT-CARE

SURPRISE GIFT CLUB

We've all faced the problem of what to give someone as a gift. Finally there's help. The Surprise Gift of the Month Club has developed an innovative solu-

tion. They will offer you a broad selection of items from kites, iron ons, coasters, stickers, records, crewel and needlepoint kits and many more items to select from. Anyone young or old will be delighted to receive a gift each month. It's a nice way to say "I'm thinking of you" to someone special. For a sample of the assorted crewel and needlepoint kits, send $1.00 for postage and handling to:

SURPRISE GIFT OF THE MONTH CLUB
PO BOX 11
GARNERVILLE, NY 10923
On the web: www.myfree.com

ELDERHOSTEL

Elderhostel offers moderately priced learning vacations across the United States and Canada as well as 45 nations abroad for senior citizens who enjoy adventure and travel but who have a limited amount of money to spend. The subjects taught on these vacations range from astronomy, to zoology. For a catalog of courses and travel itineraries, write:

ELDERHOSTEL
11 AVENUE DE LAFAYETTE
BOSTON, MA. 02111-1746
OR CALL 1-877-426-8056
WWW.ELDERHOSTEL.ORG

FREE HELP CHOOSING THE RIGHT COLLEGE

Selecting the right college or university can be a challenging and time-consuming task but one that will bring immeasurable rewards for the rest of your life. To help you make the right choice, State Farm Insurance has a fantastic guide from U.S. News and World Report. In its close to 300 pages you will find valuable information about tuition, room and board, financial aid, entrance requirements and lots more on over 1,400 universities and colleges. To get your free copy of this important guide, call State Farm toll-free at:

1-888-733-8368

HOUSE OF ONYX

If you like gems and gemstones...whether in the

rough or finished into fine jewelry or artifacts, this catalog is for you. You will find some fabulous close-out buys on some fantastic gemstones, geodes even Mexican onyx and malachite carvings. If you are just a collector or need some great gifts, send for this catalog. Write:

HOUSE OF ONYX
THE AARON BUILDING
120 NORTH MAIN ST.
GREENVILLE, KY 42345-1504
WWW.HOUSEOFONYX.COM

HOME BUYING

Are you considering buying a house? If so this is a must. You will receive *The American Homeowner's Foundation's Top 10 Homebuyers Tips.* They'll also include *Top 10 Remodeling Tips.* Call The American Homeowners Foundation at: 1-800-489-7776
Or visit their web site at:
www.americanhomeowners.org

CONSUMER GEM KIT

Buying a valuable gem can be a tricky affair unless you are prepared. Have you ever wondered what makes one diamond more valuable than another that may look the same to the naked eye? Before buying any gemstone it is essential to learn exactly what to look for. For example do you know the 4 'C's' that determine a diamond's value? They are... Cut... Color... Clarity... Carat (weight). To learn more about what to look for when buying a diamond, send for a free consumer kit from the American Gem Society. Send a card to:

THE AMERICAN GEM SOCIETY
8881 W. SAHARA AVE.
LAS VEGAS, NV 89117
Visit them on the web at: www.ags.org

SLEEP TIGHT

A healthful good night's sleep makes for a very productive, pleasant person. Learn all the facts on how to get a healthful sleep, by selecting the right bedding pillows and positions. The makers of Simmons will send you this free book *Consumer Guide To Better Sleep* plus several others including *It's Never Too Early To Start Caring For Your Back* and tips for shopping for the right bed. Send a business-sized SASE to:

SIMMONS BEAUTYREST
ONE CONCOURSE CENTER, SUITE 600
BOX C-93
ATLANTA, GA 30328

KNIFE SHOWPLACE

This catalog with hundreds of knives, swords specialty and novelty knives, sharpening systems, accessories, etc. will help you find that special carving knife for apples, cheese or fruitcake. If you are a collector of swords and sheaths there are a few to choose from. Write:

SMOKY MOUNTAIN KNIFE WORKS
BOX 4430
SEVIERVILLE, TN 37864

HAPPY CHILD - HAPPY ADULT

Parenting is difficult. Sometimes you need to take a few minute 'time out' to calm yourself down before disciplining your child. Next time you feel like hitting your child, try another approach. For example you might do something like making an origami paper hat, or any game that gives you the time you need to cool off. Remember the time it takes to make a paper hat could keep you from hurting your child. For this excellent free book write:

"PREVENTING CHILD ABUSE"
PO BOX 2866 P
CHICAGO, IL 60690

MONEY SAVING TIPS

Here's a great newsletter loaded with information in the form of handy, easy-to-understand tips, on the all important topics of saving both time and money. You'll also find an assortment of quick and easy recipe ideas and the *Frugal Mom* weekly newsletter. You'll find them online at:

www.thefamilycorner.com

LOVE LETTER NEWSLETTER

Love guru, Greg Godek, author of the bestselling book, *1001 Ways To Be More Romantic*, would like to give you a free one year subscription to LoveLetter Newsletter, chuck full of great romantic ideas. Put the spark back in your love life. Call Casablance Press at:
1-800-43-BRIGHT **(1-800-432-7444)**
Or visit them on the web at:www.sourcebooks.com

NEWS FOR YOU

This freebie is for adults whose reading levels is grade 4 to 6, and is a great way to help improve their skills. Each issue contains articles covering important international news as well as features on education, health, leisure, law, etc. To get a free issue, ask for *News For You Sample Copy*. Write to:
NEW READERS PRESS
PO BOX 35888
SYRACUSE, NY 13235
1-800-448-8878
www.newreaderspress.com

FASHION EASE

Fashion Ease specializes in clothing for elderly, arthritic or handicapped people. Styles wrap and close easily with Velcro or snaps. There are wheelchair accessories and items for the incontinent. To get a copy of their free catalog, write to:
FASHION EASE
541 6TH ST.
BROOKLYN, NY 11219

SMART WIGS

For the best prices on the finest wigs, send for this free catalog. You will be amazed at the beautiful selection of wigs from Revlon, Adolfo and many more. So if you are in the market for a wig write to:
BEAUTY TREND
PO BOX 9323, DEPT. 44002
HIALEAH, FL 33014

ART FILMS

To help bring art appreciation to a wider audience The National Gallery of Art would like to send you a film without charge. They have dozens of films and slide programs to lend to individuals, community groups, schools, etc. Your only obligation is to pay the postage when sending the film back. For a complete *catalog and reservation card* send a card to:

NATIONAL GALLERY OF ART
EXTENSION PROGRAM
WASHINGTON, DC 20565
Visit them on the web at: www.nga.gov

HEALTHY HOME HOTLINE

To help make housework easier and less time consuming, Bounty has developed their new Rinse & Reuse paper towel that keeps its strength when wet allowing you to reuse the towel. You'll receive a sample plus the booklet, *The New Rules of Cleaning* with cleaning tips. Just call:

1-888-4-NEW-RULES

FOR THE LARGER-SIZED OR TALLER WOMAN

Lane Bryant offers a stunning collection of dresses, coats, jeans, sportswear, lingerie and shoes to the woman who wears half size or large size apparel. You'll find name brands and designer fashions in their free *catalog*. If you are 5'7" or taller also ask for their *Tall Collection catalog*. call:

LANE BRYANT, **1-800-677-0216**
OR VISIT THEM ON THE WEB AT:
www.lbcatalog.com

SHOP EASY

Relax and shop at home. Lillian Vernon's *free catalog is* full of affordable treasures from all around the world. Call:

LILLIAN VERNON
1-800-545-5426

OR VISIT THEM ON THE WEB AT:
www.lillianvernon.com

CLASSIC GIFTS

Harriet Carter has provided distinctive gifts since 1958. This fun-filled catalog is chuck-full of unique gifts you will find fascinating. Write to:
HARRIET CARTER
425 STUMP RD
NORTH WALES, PA 19454
OR VISIT THGEM ON THE WEB AT:
WWW.HARRIETCARTER.COM

GET THAT BUG

The makers of Raid bug sprays would like you to have a highly informative chart, *Raid Insecticides - What to Use For Effective Control.* Learn how to deal with crawling, flying and biting pests both inside and outside your home (including plant pests). You'll also receive a money-saving coupon. Send a postcard to:
"INSECT CONTROL"
S C JOHNSON
1525 HOWE STREET
RACINE, WI 53403-5011
1-800-494-4855
www.johnsonwax.com

COOPERATIVE EXTENSION

Your local cooperative extension office offers an amazing range of free information and services to all who request them. Soil analysis, 4-H information, home economics classes and money-management workshops are just a few of the services available. Call your local Extension Service. It's listed under "County Government" in the phone book.

HOME BUYING

If you are thinking of buying an older home any time in the near future, there are certain things you should do to protect yourself. For example before buying the home, it is a good idea to hire a trained inspector to check for defects you might not see such as termites or a roof in need of repair. Be sure to get a copy of *Tips For Buying a Good Older Home.* Send a long SASE to:

NATIONAL INSPECTION SERVICES
1136 EAST STUART ST. SUITE 4204
FORT COLLINS, CO 80525
CALL THEM TOLL-FREE AT: 800-248-1976
Or vist them online at: www.nationalinspection.net

CONSUMER COMPLAINTS

If you ever wanted to complain to a company about one of their products but didn't know how to go about it, this is for you. *How To Talk To A Company And Get Action* should help you get your problem solved—fast. You'll also receive the "Story of Coca Cola". Write to:

CONSUMER INFORMATION CENTER
COCA-COLA CO.
DEPT. FR, P.O. DRAWER 1734
ATLANTA, GA 30301

WELCOME ADDITION

If you have recently had a baby and need breast milk storage bottles, gel packs for diaper packs, etc. be sure to get a copy of the Ross Materials Catalog. Write to:

ROSS PRODUCTS
625 CLEVELAND AVE.
COLUMBUS, OH 43215
1-800-986-8510
www.similac.com

GERBER BABY

Whether you are a new parent or just looking for some helpful tips Gerber has a great book *Feeding Your Baby*. This handy guide gives you practical tips for feeding your baby from birth to age three. So your baby will learn healthful eating habits right from the start. You'll also receive some money savings coupons to get you started. Ask for the Gerber baby care package. Call:

1-800-4-GERBER (THAT'S 1-800-443-7237)

FINDING THE RIGHT CAMP OR SCHOOL

Choosing the right sleepaway camp or private school

can be very confusing. To help take the confusion out of camp or school shopping here's a helpful booklet, *How To Choose A Camp For Your Child.* Send a SASE to:
AMERICAN CAMPING ASSN.
5000 STATE RD.
67 NORTH
MARTINSVILLE, IN 46151

BOYS & GIRLS CLUBS OF AMERICA

Give your boys things to do and a place to go to develop their character. The Boys Clubs of America have been doing this for over 100 years. They have 1100 local chapters in 700 towns. Ask for the *Boy's & Girl's Club Information Package.* Write to:
BOYS & GIRLS CLUB OF AMERICA
3 WEST 35TH STREET
NEW YORK, NY 10001

THE COMPANY STORE

If you are looking for a superior blend of hand selected white goose and duck down feather comforters, pillows or outerwear this is the place for you. Drop a postcard for their *free catalog* to:
THE COMPANY STORE
500 COMPANY STORE ROAD
LA GROSSE, WI 54601
WWW.THECOMPANYSTORE.COM

WORDS OF WISDOM

If you need words of encouragement to keep going in the face of adversity (and who doesn't), *Portrait of An Achiever* is an inspirational addition to any home. This beautiful parchment reproduction is suitable for framing and makes an excellent gift. Send $1.00 s&h to:
ROBLIN PRESS
405 TARRYTOWN RD SUITE 414 - POA
WHITE PLAINS, NY 10607

MAIL ORDER BUYING

Here is a practical and informative guide detailing the protection you have under the FTC's Mail Order Merchandise Rule. A free copy of *Shopping By Phone & Mail* is yours by writing to:

SHOPPING BY PHONE AND MAIL
CONSUMER RESPONSE CENTER
FEDERAL TRADE COMMISSION
600 PENN. AVENUE NW, ROOM H130
WASHINGTON, DC 20580
Or visit them on the web at: www.ftc.org

YOUR OWN FLAG OVER THE CAPITOL

Your Congressman will provide a unique service for you free of charge. If you'd like to have your own flag flown over the U.S. Capitol Building write to your congressman. The flag itself is not free (prices range from $16.00 to $31.00 depending upon size and material) but the service of having the flag purchased, flown and sent to you is free. This also makes a unique gift for someone special. Write to your own Congressperson at:

US HOUSE OF REPRESENTITIVES
WASHINGTON, DC 20515
OR
US SENATE
WASHINGTON, DC 20510

PRESERVE OUR HISTORY

If you'd like to participate in the preservation of sites, buildings and objects that are important to American history and culture, there is something you can do. Drop a card asking for the *Historic Preservation package* to:

NATIONAL TRUST FOR HISTORIC PRESERVATION
1785 MASSACHUSETTS AVE. N.W.
WASHINGTON, DC 20036
www.nthp.org

CONSUMER HANDBOOK

A problem everyone has at one time or another is who to turn to when he has a complaint. Now with the *Consumer Resource Handbook* you will know the best non-government and government sources to contact for help. This is something no one should be without. Send a card to:

CONSUMER RESOURCE HANDBOOK
CONSUMER INFORMATION CENTER
PUEBLO, CO 91009

YOUR OWN MONEYTREE

Wouldn't it be great to have your very own moneytree growing in a corner of your kitchen? Well maybe you can. American companies give away billions of dollars of gifts, cash, sweepstakes and freebies every year. The editors of *MoneyTree Digest* will show you how to get your share of the Great American Giveaway. To get a sample issue of this terrific magazine, send $1.00 postage & handling to:

MONEYTREE DIGEST
648 CENTRAL AVE. SUITE 441-BFT
SCARSDALE, NY 10583

POPCORN PANDEMONIUM

Love popcorn? Ready for something different? Why not try rum butter toffee, peanut butter, fruit salad or cinnamon flavored popcorn? The Popcorn Factory has everything you ever dreamed of in popcorn, jelly beans, pretzels, nuts and home poppers. For a free catalog, call them at:
1-800-541-2676

BUYING LIFE INSURANCE

Buying the right amount and the right type of life insurance is one of the important decisions you must make. Before you make any decision, be sure to get your copy of *How To Choose A Life Insurance Company*. To get your copy of this informative booklet, simply send a postcard to:
OCCIDENTAL LIFE
BOX 2101 TERMINAL ANNEX
LOS ANGELES, CA 90051

FLAGS

If you are looking for any kind of flag, poles and accessories, including custom designs, state's, nation's, historic, nautical...you name it... this *free catalog* has them all. Visit them at their web site:
www.qualityflags.com

CHAPPED LIPS?

If you suffer from dry chapped lips or mouth sores, this is especially for you. You will receive sample packets of Blistex Lip Ointment plus two informative brochures and a 25¢-off coupon too. Send a long SASE to:

BLISTEX SAMPLE OFFER
1800 SWIFT DR.
OAK BROOK, IL 60521

LOVE FRAGRANCES

If you love all those expensive perfumes and colognes advertised on TV, radio and magazines but don't want to pay the high prices, this is a must for you. For your free list and scented cards, drop a card to:

ESSENTIAL PRODUCTS CO. INC.
90 WATER ST.
NEW YORK, NY 10005

"SCHOOL ZONE"

If you are a parent, you want to help build a solid foundation of important basic skills for your child. This *free catalog* will help you encourage learning and prepare your child for the future. Write:

SCHOOL ZONE PUBLISHING
PO BOX 777
GRAND HAVEN, MI 49417

KEEP WARM

Stay warm this winter with insulated clothing, outdoor equipment and toasty down comforters that you make yourself — with the help of a Frostline kit. For a copy of their free catalog, send a postcard to:

FROSTLINE KITS
2525 RIVER ROAD.
GRAND JUNCTION, CO 81505

DECIDED TO MOVE?

How To Stretch Your Moving Budget – The Interstate Moving Guide is a useful pamphlet that will help you make your interstate move run smoothly. It tells you how to prepare for moving day, how moving costs are calculated, a glossary of moving terms

and lots more. It's your free from:
ATLAS VAN LINES
1212 ST. GEORGE RD.
EVANSVILLE, IN 47711-2364
1-800-252-8885
www.atlasvanlines.com

A MOVING EXPERIENCE

To help you with your next move United Van Lines has set up a toll free number you can call. Their local offices are set up to answer any specific questions you may have. For example, they can find answers to your questions about employment, educational facilities, housing, and more, in 7,000 cities and towns throughout the 50 states (and foreign countries too). They can also provide you with guides which make preplanning a lot easier and they'll give you the local phone number of the United Van Lines nearest you. Call:
1-877-317-4636
UNITED VAN LINES
ONE UNITED DR.
FENTON, MO 63026
www.unitedvanlines.com

PLANNING A MOVE

Mayflower has a nice packet of moving materials free for the asking. It includes labels to mark your boxes with plus tips to make your move run smoother and faster. Ask for your *"Moving Kit"* from your local Mayflower mover or send a card to:
MAYFLOWER MOVERS
ONE MAYFLOWER DRIVE
FENTON, MO 63026
www.mayflowertransit.com

SHIPS AND THE SEA

This 100 page *catalog is* full of decorative nautical ideas for the home. If you're looking for a ship model, marine painting or ship's wheel you'll find it here. Drop a postcard to:
S. T. PRESTON & SON
MAIN ST. WHARF
GREENPORT, NY 11944
OR VISIT THEM ON THE WEB AT: WWW.PRESTONS.COM

FREE GIFT FROM THE PRESIDENT

Imagine the excitement of getting a letter from the President of the United States. The President will send a signed letter embossed with the Presidential seal to any couple celebrating their 50th anniversary (or beyond) or to any citizen celebrating their 80th (or subsequent) birthday. At the other end of the spectrum, the President will also send a congratulatory card to any newborn child. What a great gift!! Send (or fax) your requests at least 6 weeks in advance to:

THE GREETINGS OFFICE
THE WHITE HOUSE
WASHINGTON, DC 20502-0039
FAX: 1-202-456-2461
WWW.WHITEHOUSE.GOV/GREETING

FREE FROM THE WHITE HOUSE

The President would like you to have a beautiful full color book called: *The White House, The House of The People.* It features a room-by-room photo tour and history of the White House. For your free copy write to:

THE WHITE HOUSE
1600 PENNYSLVANIA AVE. NW
WASHINGTON, DC 20502
OR REQUEST IT BY FAX: 1-202-456-2461

FREE PHOTO OF THE PRESIDENT

How would you like a beautiful photo of the President of the U.S. and the First Lady? To get your free photo, request it by fax at:

1-202-456-2461 Or write to:
WHITE HOUSE GREETINGS OFFICE
1600 PENNSYLVANIA **NW**
WASHINGTON, **DC 20502-0039**

THE PRESIDENT WANTS YOUR OPINION

No matter what your opinion on how the country is being run, the President is interested in knowing how you feel. So no matter whether you agree or disagree with current policies, call the special number that will take directly to the White House where you will be able to express your opinion.. Call:
1-202-456-1111

HAIR REMOVAL

If you're a woman with unsightly body hair, this is for you. 'Hers' is a full line of products that deal with the sensitive issue of hair removal treatments. Visit their web site at:
www.nudit.com

CHILDREN AND VIOLENCE

In today's society children are exposed to the medias hype of violence and horror stories. There are several warning signs to help us recognize and prevent any violence children may be exposed to. The American Psychological Association and MTV, publish an excellent guide called *Warning Signs*, to help us discuss these issues with our children before they get out of hand. For a free copy of *Warning Signs*, call:
1-800-268-0078

CYBER SAFETY

Parents know to buckle up their kids before driving on the highway but what can they do to keep them safe on the information highway...the Internet? The U.S. Department Of Education publishes a great guide to help you set rules for your children's Internet use and to be aware of their activities online. The Internet can offer an invaluable source of information for your child if he or she is looking for specific information, however there may also be offensive and off-limit sites that you should be aware of. Today computer technology changes so fast that the more informed parents are the better

equipped they are to point out safe sites for their kids. Ask for *Parents Guide to the Internet.* To get your free copy, call:
1-800-USA-LEARN (THAT's **1-800-872-5327**)

PET ALLERGIES

If you are allergic to pets there may be a new way to eliminate those allegies around the house with a new vacuum by Nilfisk, Inc. of America. Call:
1-800-241-9420 Ext **2**

HERE ARE A FEW TOLL-FREE HOTLINES YOU CAN CALL FOR SPECIAL UP-TO-THE MINUTE INFORMATION ON IMPORTANT TOPICS

HEADACHE HOTLINE

The American Council for Headache Education may offer a solution on how to lessen your pain and discomfort
1-800-255-ACHE

ASTHMA INFORMATION

If you or your child suffers from asthma, you will want to get a free copy of the *Asthma & Allergy Information package.* You will discover what you can do to assist your doctor in helping you relieve asthma suffering. If you have a child with asthma, ask for the free *Child Care Asthma / Allergy Action Card.* Call them toll-free:
1-800-7-ASTHMA (THAT's 1-800-727-8462)
or visit their excellent web site:
www.aafa.org

CARPET CARE

If you are thinking of adding or changing carpets in your home but are confused by the many choices you have to make, call The Carpet and Rug Institute information line for answers to your questions related to carpeting your home
1-800-882-8846

MAKING YOUR HOME SAFE

If you would like to make your home a safer place to live, be sure to get the *Danger In The Home-- How To Make Your Home A Healthy Home For Children.* You'll find a checklist which will show you how to make every room of your home, from the kitchen to the bedroom safer. You will also find useful toll-free numbers you can call for help with health problems like respiratory illnesses, childhood lead poisoning and safe drinking water. To get your free safety poster, call:
1-800-HUDS-FHA

PEACE CORPS

The Peace Corps can give you the chance to immerse yourself in a totally different culture while helping to make an important difference in other people's lives. If you like helping people and want to get involved, be sure to get the *Peace Corps Information package.* Call toll-free:
1-800-424-8580

THE WORKING WOMAN'S WEDDING PLANNER

If you are currently planning a wedding, the folks at State Farm Insurance will send you this excellent 300 page guide . This extensive guide touches on every topic you've ever thought when it comes to your wedding. You'll get important tips on preparing a budget to planning an engagement party, to considering important insurance coverages you may need. It has numerous checklists and even provides you with a six-month calendar! So let the count down begin.
Call State Farm toll-free at:
1-888-733-8368

CARING FOR ELDERLY PARENTS

Are you faced with the dilemma of possibly caring for elderly parents - then you have lots of questions about medicare, medicaid, power of attorney and making or planning medical decisions. The National Academy of Elder Law Attorneys offers free brochures that address these complicated issues: Medicaid, Medicare, Durable Power of Attorney and Planning for Medical Decision Making. To receive all four brochures, send a long SASE to:

NATIONAL ACADEMY OF ELDER LAW ATTORNEYS
1604 N. COUNTRY CLUB RD. DEPT. FC
TUCSON, AZ 85716-3102

If you need an attorney devoted to elder law, call your local state bar association or check out NAELA's web site:

www.naela.org

ENJOY CAMPING?

If you are a person who just loves the great outdoors, you are certain to enjoy the outdoor tips and advice found in this newsletter. Be sure to visit their web site at:

www.wildernessaccess.co

Music

HUGE MUSIC & ELECTRONICS CATALOG

J & R Music World's catalog with over 10,000 products is actually one of the most comprehensive product source books in the audio, video, computer and electronics field. It features all major brand names – everything in home entertainment. For a free copy of this 304 page catalog, call toll-free: **(800) 221-8180** or send a postcard to:

J & R Music World
23 Park Row
New York, NY 10038

HOHNER HARMONICAS

Hohner, probably the best known name in harmonicas (including one that's 2 feet long) would like you to have a copy of *How to Play the Hohner Harmonica.* It is a step-by-step concise guide and song book. It also shows how to get special effects from your harmonica. For your free copy write:

M. Hohner, Inc.
PO Box 15035
Richmond, VA 23227

INTEREST YOUR CHILD IN MUSIC

Getting a youngster interested in playing a musical instrument can be quite a chore for a parent. *How Music Can Bring You Closer To Your Child* may make that task a little easier. Yours free from:

G. Leblanc Corp.
7019 30th Ave.
Kenosha, WI 53141

ELECTRIC GUITARS & MORE

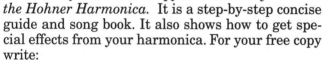

If you would like to see some of the most innovative and finely crafted electronic instruments on the market today, a free 84 page full color catalog is yours for the asking. You'll find electric guitars, amplifiers, mixers and more all available at direct-from-the-factory' prices. Write to:

Carvin Guitars
12340 World Trade Drive
San Diego, CA 92128

Craft & Hobbies

FREE BEAD SUPPLY CATALOG

If you're looking for an interesting and challenging hobby, the Frantz Bead Company has put together an informative newsletter and supply catalog to teach you the art of bead making. You'll receive a free newsletter plus a catalog with a full assortment of terrific bead supplies. Send a postcard to:

Frantz Bead Company
1222 Sunset Hill Road
Shelton, WA 98584
www.frantzartglass.com

BEAUTIFUL CHRISTMAS ORNAMENT

If you love to collect truly unique Christmas ornaments, you will definitely want to get this one. It's a beautiful hand-made angel that will quickly become the center piece of your holiday decorations. Simply send $2.00 (or 7 loose first class stamps) for shipping and handling and request the *Christmas Angel* from:

Valerie's Hattery
13435 South Cedar Road
Cedar, MI 49621

STAR SEARCH

Do you have a favorite recording artist or special movie star? Well here's your chance to get an autograph of that famous star. You'll recieve a listing of over 100 superstar names and addresses along with a brief bio and well as helpful hints on making your star search productive. Send a long SASE to:

Jim Weaver's autographs in the mail
322 Mall Blvd., #345
Monroeville, PA 15146-2229

"HOT SHOTS WITH ANY CAMERA"

This 48 page guide in full color shows you how to take the best snapshots under any circumstances. It's easy to understand and deals with topics such

as lighting, flash photography, action and more. So start taking better pictures now. Ask for *Hot Shots With Any Camera.* Call toll-free: **1-800-242-2424**

PLAYING BETTER CHESS

Chess helps you develop your ability to think analytically. Now you can learn the official rules of this challenging game of chess and also receive another publication to join the U.S. Chess Federation. Ask for *Ten Tips To Winning Chess.* Send a SASE to:
U.S. CHESS FEDERATION
3054 NYS ROUTE 9W
NEW WINDSOR, NY 12553
OR CALL: 1-800-388-5464
www.shopuschess.org

THE ART OF VENTRILOQUISM

Here is your chance to learn about what a ventriloquist is and how to become one. You will also learn how to build a puppet and even put together and market a show. You will learn how to start, the direction to go in and more. Remember Howdy Doody, and Edgar and Jerry Mahoney? Well you can learn all the same techniques they used. To receive this 32 page booklet on how to become a ventriloquist write to :
THE NORTH AMERICAN ASSOCIATION OF VENTRILOQUISTS
BOX 420
LITTLETON CO 80160
Or visit their web site at: www.maherstudios.com/ naav.htm

BLACK JACK"

A free Black Jack Strategy Card is yours for the asking. This pocket-sized card gives you invaluable strategies, based on what you are dealt and what the tester is showing. Various combinations of hands and dealer show cards are printed right on an easy to read chart. Gambling ...blackjack in particular...can be fun if you're able to combine luck with a little strategy. Ask for *Black Jack Strategy Card* write to:
THOMAS GAMING SERVICES
PO BOX 1383
GOLETA, CA 93116

CROCHET TIME

These free crochet instructions will show you how to make some beautiful hand made ornaments, that you could sell, give as gifts or enjoy yourself. You can make seven simple thread snowflakes and 10 easy yarn ornaments. So get started now and send for your free instructions. Ask for *Crochet Tree-Trim Pattern*. Send a SASE to:

LORRAINE VETTER-BFT
7924 SOPER HILL ROAD
EVERETT, WA 98205

HOME SEWING BASICS

If you're thinking of decorating anything from a single room to an entire house, be sure to get *Sewing - It's Sew Soothing*. Discover how much fun it is to make your own curtains, slip covers and pillow shams. To get your copy, send a long SASE to:

HOME SEWING ASSOCIATION
1350 BROADWAY SUITE 1601
NEW YORK, NY 10018
www.sewing.org

POLAROID PROBLEMS?

Have your Polaroid photos been coming out the way you'd like? There's a toll-free hotline to call where an expert will answer any questions you may have. Call toll free 8am -8pm Mon- Sat. at **800-343-5000.** Polaroid has a commendable policy of complete customer satisfaction. Your problem may lie with defective film which they'll replace at no charge. Send defective film or photos to:

POLAROID CUSTOMER CARE SERVICE
201 BURLINGTON ROAD
BEDFORD, MA 01730
www.polaroid.com

PICTURE THIS

Kodak has a great web site that will help you take better photos. You will find... Top 10 techniques for good photos; Problem-pictures remedies; Picture taking tips for any situation plus a host of other topics and chat rooms relating to digital, general and professional photography.

Visit their web site at:
WWW.KODAK.COM

HOW TO MAKE PLAY CLAY

Create your own gifts, decorations and jewelry with play clay. You'll learn how to make play clay from Arm & Hammer Baking Soda. When you write, ask for *"Play Clay brochures"*. Drop a card to:

ARM & HAMMER CONSUMER RELATIONS
PLAY CLAY BROCHURES
PO BOX 1625
HORSHAM, PA 19044-6625
1-800-524-1328
WWW.ARMHAMMER.COM

BEAUTIFUL LETTERS

If you are interested in learning how to create handcrafted lettering, this is for you. With the *Hunt Lettering Charts* you will receive a super collection of Roman Gothic, Old English and Manuscript lettering charts plus helpful hints. Send a card to:

SPEEDBALL ART PRODUCTS
PO BOX 5157
2226 SPEEDBALL ROAD
STATESVILLE, NC 28677
WWW.SPEEDBALLART.COM

PICTURE PERFECT

Kodak has a freebie for all of you who want to take those perfect pictures. Give them a call and ask for *365 Days to Better Pictures,* call:
1-800-599-5929

PLAYING DUPLICATE BRIDGE

If you're a Bridge player, you'll want this catalog and product source guide. Write to:

AMERICAN CONTRACT BRIDGE LEAGUE
2990 AIRWAYS BLVD.
P.O. BOX 161192
MEMPHIS, TN 38116
1-800-467-2623
WWW.ACBL.ORG

ZIPPO COLLECTORS

Somewhere in your attic or basement you my stumble across an old Zippo lighter, known for their reliability and quality for over 50 years. To find out whether your old Zippo has any real value today,

ask for a copy of *Collectors Guide* :
ZIPPO MANUFACTURING CO.
33 BARBOUN ST.
BRADFORD, PA 16701
WWW.ZIPPO.COM

BRIDAL ANGELS

Do you collect angels? If so, this lovely Bridal Angel is a must. She comes with her own rose bouquet, floral and silver bead headpiece and necklace. It's made from natural muslin, you can hang it up as a decoration or give it to a new bride to be as a gift. The birds nest bouquet even has tiny roses and mini streamers. Ask for the *Guardian Bridal Angel* (it makes a great holiday angel too!) Send six first class stamps to:

VALERIE'S HATTERY
13435 SOUTH CEDAR ROAD
CEDAR, MI 49621

OLD-TIME STAMPS

There's an old-time collection of 26 different stamps waiting for you. Each stamp is 50 to 100 years old. The stamps are worth $3.00 at catalog prices but are yours for only 50 cents postage. You'll also receive other stamps on approval but there's no obligation to buy anything. Write to:

JAMESTOWN STAMP CO,
341 EAST 3RD STREET
JAMESTOWN, NY 14701
1-888-782-6776
www.jamestownstamp.com

START A STAMP CLUB

If you're interested in collecting stamps you might enjoy the company of other stamp collectors. For a free copy of *You Can Start A Stamp Club*. Write to:
AMERICAN PHILATELIC SOCIETY
P.O. BOX 8000
STATE COLLEGE, PA 16803
WWW.STAMPS.ORG

NUMISMATIC NEWS

Here's a newspaper coin collectors will want to have. Simply write and request a free copy of *Numismatic Weekly*. You'll enjoy its many interesting articles.

Send a card to:
NUMISMATIC NEWS WEEKLY
KRAUSE PUBLICATIONS
700 EAST STATE STREET
IOLA, WI 54990
1-800-258-0929
WWW.KRAUSE.COM

COMIC BOOK COLLECTORS

If you enjoy collecting old comic books, you will want to send for a giant list of back issues of Marvel comics. Send 50¢ postage to:
R. CRESTOHL
4732 CIRCLE RD.
MONTREAL, CANADA

U.S. COINS

U.S. nickels and pennies haven't always looked as they look now. You'll receive one buffalo nickel and four 'wheat' pennies -all nearly over fifty years old. To get yours, print the words *buffalo nickel and four wheat pennies* on a sheet of paper. Don't forget to include a long self-addressed stamped envelope and $1.00 (no checks please) to the address below.

BUFFALO NICKEL

Did you know that over fifty years ago nickels used to feature buffaloes? Don't believe it? Order your buffalo nickel today to start or add to your coin collection. To order yours simply print the words *buffalo nickel* on a sheet of paper , and send that along with a long self-addressed stamped envelope and 50 cents (no checks please) to the address below:

MERCURY DIME

From 1916 to1945, dimes bore the image of Mercury, the Roman god of commerce and travel. Now Mercury dimes are rare - in fact, they're considered collectors' items. Add one to your collection! To get yours, print the words *mercury dime* on a sheet of paper and send that with a long self-addressed stamped envelope and $1.00 (no checks please) to the address below:
EDINBORO CREATIONS
DEPT 1
1210 BRIERLY LANE
MUNHALL, PA 15120

For Pet Lovers

MORE THAN A FRIEND

To millions of people their pet is a real member of the family. And love of animals has inspired many to follow a career path to becoming a veterinarian. For these people the American Veterinary Association has an interesting booklet called *"Today's Veterinarian"* about the opportunities available today in this interesting field. For your free copy send a postcard to:

AMERICAN VETERINARY ASSOCIATION
1931 NORTH MEECHAM RD. SUITE 100,
SCHAUMBURG, IL 60173
WWW.AVMA.ORG

CARING FOR A NEW PUPPY OR KITTEN

If you're thinking of getting a new puppy or kitten this freebie from Iams Company is for you. *You & Your New Puppy* and *You & Your New Kitten* give you useful advice on feeding, house-training, health care, grooming, training of a new pet and more. Write to:

THE IAMS COMPANY
PUPPY/KITTEN INFORMATION CENTER
BOX 1475
DAYTON, OHIO 45401

GAINES FOODS

Gaines foods has a number of informative publications that are yours for the asking. Write for the free publications list to:

QUAKER PROFESSIONAL SERVICES
585 HAWTHORNE COURT #14
GALESBURG, IL 61401

PET CARE & NUTRITION

If you'd like any information about proper pet care and pet nutrition, the makers of Kal Kan pet food would like to help you. They will send you *"Understanding Your Dog"* and *"Understanding Your Cat."* Write to:

KAL KAN CONSUMER ADVISORY SERVICE
3386 EAST 44TH ST.
P.O. BOX 58853
VERNON, CA 90058

CARING FOR YOUR PET

If you have a dog or are planning to get one, make sure you write for *free pet information.* The folks at Ralston Purina dog food products have an excellent freebie that will not only give you a brief history of dogs, but also give you tips on feeding your dog, grooming, obedience training, keeping your dog healthy and traveling with your dog. They may also include discount coupons and a Purina dog food guide to balancing nutrients to meet your dog's needs. Also ask for *Guide To Caring For Your Dog* and *Help! My Pet Refuses To Eat.* These freebies are a must if you've ever thought of getting a dog for a pet. Write to:

RALSTON PURINA
DOG FOOD DIVISION
CHECKERBOARD SQUARE
ST. LOUIS, MO 63164.
1-800-778-7462
www.purina.com

FOR THE BIRDS

Lafeber's Avi-Cakes Gourmet Bird Food will provide a perfectly nutritious snack to satisfy bird munchies. Avi-Cakes are a nutritionally complete bird treat with proper vitamins and delicious flavors. Get your free trial size sample now. Ask for *Avi-Cakes Sample* Write to:

LAFEBER COMPANY
24981 NORTH 1400 EAST ROAD
CORNELL, IL 61319

FISH ARE FUN

Fish are educational, fun and something the whole family can enjoy. Now you can learn step-by-step

how to set up a year round backyard pond and stock it with hardy fish. Send for your free *We Are The Water Garden Experts*. Drop a postcard to:
TETRA POND
3001 COMMERCE ST.
BLACKSBURG, VA 24060-6671
1-800-526-0650
www.tetra-fish.com

ARE YOU ALLERGIC TO DOGS?

If you would love to have a dog but can't because you are allergic, this may be your lucky day. Check out this web site where you'll find information on breeds of dogs that produce little or no allergic reaction.
Visit them at: **http://members.aol.com/AHTerrier/allergies.html**

CARE FOR YOUR PETS

The American Humane Association has a whole series of informative booklets available for pet owners. These booklets tell how to care for dogs, cats, horses, birds and fish. For a complete listing, write for their free *catalog of publications*. From:
AMERICAN HUMANE ASSOCIATION
63 INVERNESS DRIVE
ENGLEWOOD, CO 80112
1-800-227-4645
WWW.AMERICANHUMANE.ORG

ANIMAL CALENDAR AND DATEBOOK

For pet lovers everywhere, The Animal Protection Institute has a handy informative *Animals Calendar and Datebook*. In addtion to being a datebook and calendar it is full of hundreds of fascinating facts about animals plus a listing of important animal events. If you love animals, this is definitely for you. Write to:
ANIMAL PROTECTION INSTITUTE
1122 S STREET
SACRAMENTO, CA 95814
1-800-348-PETS
WWW.API4ANIMALS.ORG

Free Cookbooks

The companies giving away these free cookbooks and recipe collections do so at great expense as their way of saying "thank you" to their loyal customers. They also hope to inspire you to even greater use of their products by showing you new and innovative ways of using them to create meals you and your family will enjoy. It is always a nice idea to mention, however briefly, how much you enjoy using their products.

A DASH OF HEALTH

If you are looking for healthy meals but don't want to compromise taste, you've got to try a recipe or two from Mrs. Dash and Molly McButter. When you call this toll-free number you will get the delicious recipes of the month using these two great tasting and healthy food additives. Call:
1-800-622-DASH

BETTER THAN BUTTER

Do you like the flavor of butter but can't take the fat and cholesterol? Then you'll want to try Butter Buds These are natural flavor granules made from real butter with no artificial ingredients. Try your free sample on vegetables, rice, noodles, potatoes or anything you want to add butter flavor to. With your free sample you will also receive a money-off coupon towards your next purchase, and a handy carrying case to carry your Butter Buds with you. To get your free sample of Butter Buds, write to:
CUMBERLAND PACKING CORP.
2 CUMBERLAND STREET
BROOKLYN, NY 11205

HOLIDAY COOKING HELP

Holiday times are family fun times and that means

food. That also means cooking crises. Fortunately now there's a variety of sources you can turn to for help solving your holiday cooking problems. The following companies are there for you to answer your cooking questions:

BUTTERBALL TURKEY TALKLINE

During the holiday season, Butterball offers you round the clock assistance in person from 7am to 5pm with automated service after hours. They offer you solutions to virtually every turkey-related need. They also offer free recipe cards with tips and money-saving coupons to every caller. Call them toll-free at:
1-800-323-4848

REYNOLDS TURKEY TIPS LINE

Call this 24-hour automated hotline for professional advice on turkey defrosting, preparation and cooking. They also offer you a free *Holiday Solutions* brochure and a packet of holiday recipes and tips. Call them at:
1-800-745-4000

PERDUE HELPLINE

Let's say it's Thanksgiving Day and you have a cooking problem. Try calling the Perdue Helpline where there are Consumer Representatives on hand to coach you through your cooking dilemmas. They also have a free booklet containing tips on safe handling of poultry. Call them at:
1-800-473-7383

OCEAN SPRAY CONSUMER HELPLINE

This service is available year-round, Monday to Friday 9am to 4pm (including Thanksgiving). Their staff will answer questions on cranberries. They also offer recipes, cooking tips, nutritional information, menu planning worksheets and product information. Call them toll-free at:
1-800-662-3263
Or visit their web site at: www.oceanspray.com

HOLIDAY BAKELINE

Land O'Lakes offers you personal help from 7am to 5pm with baking advice from the experts. They can also help you with your home baking emergencies and will send you a free booklet with baking tips and recipes. For help, call their toll-free helpline at:
1-800-782-9606

FREE HEALTHY MEAL PLANNER

If you really want to improve your health, start by filling your diet with nutritious and delicious foods. To get started on the road to eating right, the folks at Kashi would like you to visit their web site. There you'll find health & nutrition tips, meal planners, tasty recipes and weight management tips. You can even join the free Kashi Club for discount coupons. Visit their web site at:
www.kashi.com

KRAFT-Y FOOD RECIPES

Do you just love cheese cake? If so you must check out Krafts web site where you'll find thousands of great recipes plus helpful tips and techniques and health and wellness ideas. Visit this terrific web site at:
www.KraftFoods.com

PICNIC TIME

Summertime is barbecue and picnic time. There are some basics you need to follow when grilling meats safely outdoors. For tips on safe food preparation and safe food handling call the USDA Meat and Poultry Hotline: Call weekdays 10am -4pm EST:
1-800-535-4555

SIMPLE AND TASTY RECIPES

The folks at College Inn Broth have a great recipe book that will help you enhance all your dishes by using their chicken, beef & vegetable broths. Call:
1-800-55-BROTH
Or visit their web site: **www.collegeinn.com**

RECIPE FOR HEALTH

We've long known that an important key to good health is a combination of good eating habits and regular exercise. The folks at Stonyfield Farm would like to show you how to be strong and well by adding calcium-rich yogurt and proper exercise into your life. For a free *Healthy Recipe Collection* plus Stonyfield Farm money-saving coupons, call Stonyfield Farm at:

1-800-776-2697
Also, check out their web site: www.stonyfield.com

STEAK SAUCE RECIPE

Learn all the great tasting meals you can make by using A-1 Steak sauce in new and innovative ways. Ask for *A-1 Steak Sauce Recipe Book* from:
NABISCO FOODS, INC.
PO BOX 1928
EAST HANOVER, NJ 07936-1928
1-800-NABISCO

MEAT & POULTRY HOTLINE

The USDA has a meat and poultry hotline to help you with questions dealing with food safety. There are a full series of recorded answers to the most commonly asked question or if you have specific questions, you can speak with a food safety expert. Call weekdays from 10:00am–4:00pm EST to speak to a specialist. For recorded messages, you can call toll-free 24 hours a day:
1-800 535-4555
Visit them on the internet at: www.usda.gov

CHANGING COURSES

If you would like to have some really great recipes using reduced fat sour cream, ask for the *Changing Courses* recipe collection. Call toll-free:
1-800-782-9602

FROM THE KELLOGG KITCHENS

If you enjoy trying new and exciting recipes, be sure

to visit Kellogg's web site and join the Kellogg Kitchens Recipe Club. Joining is free and what it means is that Kellogg will e-mail recipes directly to you. When you visit their web site be sure to also check out their extensive collection of recipes listed by categories (like appetizers, entrees, desserts, breads and more). If you have a favorite Kellogg food, you can also check recipes by product. So no matter what foods you enjoy, you're sure to find a ton of great recipes to try.

Be sure to visit Kellogg on the web at:
www.Kellogg.com/recipes

PRIZE-WINNING BEEF RECIPES

If you would like to sample some of the best beef recipes in the nation, be sure to get a copy of the *National Beef Cook-Off Prize Winning Recipes.* You will find a host of delicious easy-to-prepare meals ranging from Chile Pizza to Gecian Skillet Ribeyes. Send a SASE to:

NATIONAL BEEF COOK-OFF RECIPES
PO BOX 3881
ENGLEWOOD, CO 80155
1-800-848-9088
Visit them on the web at: www.beefcookoff.org

DELI-DELICIOUS

Simply Sensational Suppers Recipes contains a slew of recipes for perfect party platters. Preparation times and even calorie counts accompany the recipes. This wonderful freebie comes to you from the National Live Stock and Meat Board. Ask for *Simply Sensational Suppers.* Just send a SASE to:

NATIONAL LIVE STOCK AND MEAT BOARD
444 N. MICHIGAN AVE., DEPT. EE
CHICAGO, IL 60611

WHEN IN ROME

History shows that the Romans used clay cookware centuries ago. Clay retains moisture which is released slowly during cooking resulting in savory self-basted food. For a terrific collec-

tion of recipes using clay Brique Ware, ask for *Brique Ware Recipes and Microwaving with Nordic Ware.*" Free from:
CUSTOMER SERVICE NORDIC WARE
HIGHWAY 7 AT 100
MINNEAPOLIS, MN 55416

JUST FOR DESSERT LOVERS

The ultimate cookie is here. Saco Foods will send you these ten delicious recipes plus a 20 cents off coupon. Create a chocolate sensation today with these delicious chocolate chunks. Remember it's the chocolate that counts. Now it's easy to get more sweet satisfaction in each bite! They even have a *Bake Your Best Hotline:*

1-800-373-SACO. Or send a SASE to:
SACO FOODS
PO Box 620707
MIDDLETOWN, WI 53562

HOT STUFF

Red Devil Hot Sauce is a zesty hot sauce that has dozens of uses—in soups, stews, sandwiches and just about anywhere you want to add a lively taste to your food. For a compact collection of dozens of recipes, send a postcard asking for *Seasoning With Trappey's Red Devil Hot Sauce* to:
B. F. TRAPPEY'S SONS
DRAWER 400
NEW IBERIA, LA 70560

BAKERS HOTLINE

Fleishmann's Yeast Bakers Help Line, specializes answering your questions about yeast and bread-baking, including advice on using bread machines. Call weekdays between 10 am and 8pm.
1-800-777-4959

SNAP, CRACKLE &...NUTRITION

When is a Rice Krispie more than a Rice Krispie? When it's part of a well-balanced nutrition program. The people at Kellogg's would like to show you how to serve your family more nutritious

meals. Send for *Kellogg's Favorite Recipes* free from:
DEPARTMENT OF HOME ECONOMICS
KELLOGG CO.
BATTLE CREEK, MI 49016

RICE SO NICE

Are you always in a hurry to prepare a new nutritious main dish. Call the Rice-A-Roni Main Dish Helpline. Call this computerized phone service will help you put together a great meals in less than 30 minutes. You will also receive quick to prepare rice and pasta recipes. Call **1-800-421-2444.**
Or write to:
GOLDEN GRAIN CO.
PO BOX 049003
CHICAGO, IL 60604
WEB ADDRESS: WWW.RICEARONI.COM

COOKING LIGHT

We all know that what we eat affects our health. But exactly what foods are the best for our health? How do you prepare foods that are good for you? Now there's a toll-free number you can call for answers to these and other questions you may have. This hotline sponsored by the Healthy Cooking magazine will put you in touch with registered dietitians who will answer your questions about cooking light. Call between 9 a.m. and 5:30 p.m. weekdays **1-800-231-3438**

POPPIN' FRESH DOUGH

Pillsbury brings you some prize winning recipes...cakes from scratch, easy yeast baking...all kinds of refrigerated dough ideas. All this to help make your next dessert a sweet and tasty delight. Yours free from:
PILLSBURY CO.
CONSUMER RESPONSE
2866 PILLSBURY CENTER
MINNEAPOLIS, MN 55402
Visit their web site at: www.pillsbury.com

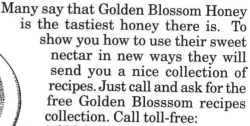

"GOLDEN BLOSSOM"

Many say that Golden Blossom Honey is the tastiest honey there is. To show you how to use their sweet nectar in new ways they will send you a nice collection of recipes. Just call and ask for the free Golden Blosssom recipes collection. Call toll-free:
1-800-220-2110
Visit their web site at:
www.goldenblossomhoney.com

GRILL-OUT

If you love to barbacue, call the Weber Grill Hotline at **1-800-GRILL-OUT** and get answers to all your barbecue questions including cooking methods, fat trimming tips and clean up to recipes, steak cooking hints and food safety tips. You'll also receive a free guide with loads of great barbecue recipes. Ask for *More Backyard Barbecue Basics*. Or visit them online at:
www.weber.com

FOOD FACTS

The Department of Agriculture has a large package of fascinating and educational materials including a handy food pyramid guide waiting for you. Learn exactly what the USDA does in the areas of consumer services, food safety, nutrition and lots more. Excellent teaching and learning tool. Write to:
U.S. DEPARTMENT OF AGRICULTURE
PUBLICATIONS DIV.
WASHINGTON, DC 20250.
OR VISIT THEIR WEB SITE AT: **www.usda.gov**

POPCORN LOVERS

If popcorn is a favorite of yours *Favorite Popcorn Recipes* is a must. It features mouth-watering popcorn balls, zesty treats and sweet 'n munchy snacks. Drop a postcard to:
AMERICAN POPCORN CO.
BOX 178
SIOUX CITY, IA 51102
Their web site is located at: www.jollytime.com

PASTA - A FOOD FOR TODAY

Here are three excellent booklets for the health conscious. There are great recipes and lots of things you can add to pasta. There are even quick microwave dishes you can make. Ask for *New World PastaRecipes* from:

NEW WORLD PASTA
CONSUMER RELATIONS
PO BOX 126457
HARRISBURG, PA 17112
1-800-730-5957
Or vist them on the web at: www.nwpasta.com

EATING HEALTHY

AARP has a nutrition guide with information on dietary guidelines, the food pyramid, the new food labels and special diets for a better quality of life. To get a free copy of *Healthy Eating For a Healthy Life* (stock #D15565), send a postcard to:

AARP FULFILLMEMNT EE0924
601 E STREET N.W.
WASHINGTON, D.C. 20049

CHEESE RECIPES

Six cheese recipes on file cards are available free from Marin French Cheese Company. Also included will be a mail order price list for their fine line of cheeses. Free from:

MARIN FRENCH CHEESE CO.
7500 RED HILL RD.
PETALUMA, CA 94952
1-800-292-6001
Visit them on the internet at:
www.marinfrenchcheese.com

DE-LIGHT TORTILLAS

To help you add a 'south of the border' touch to your next meal, the folks at Mission Foods would like to send you *The Art of Light Tortillas*. Learn how to make a delightful Spanish Pizza, Strawberry Breakfast Crepes, Fiesta Crab Crisps and lots more.

CALL TOLL FREE: 1-800-600-TACO

SWEET TOOTH

Looking for new dessert ideas your whole family will enjoy? You'll find lots of yummy dessert recipes and also learn how to cut the fat from sweets with *Plum Good* recipe. For your free copy and discount coupon, write to:

SOKOL & CO.
5315 DANSHER RD.
COUNTRYSIDE, IL 60525
1-800-328-7656

For a great collection of recipes, check out their web site at:

www.solofoods.com

BREAKFAST & MORE

Roman Meal Company makes an excellent line of whole grain breads. The *Roman recipe collection* will show you how to make meals your family will love—like Porcupine Meatballs or Sloppy Joe's. You'll also receive budget stretcher ideas and low-fat diet menus. Free from:

ROMAN MEAL CO.
PO BOX 11126
TACOMA, WA 98411
Visit them on the web at: www.romanmeal.com

APPLE SAUCE

This great cookbook has some of the most delightful recipes using Lucky Leaf Apple Sauce. You will find recipes for everything from entrees to desserts. It's yours free from:

KNOUSE FOODS
800 PEACH GLEN ROAD
PEACH GLEN, PA 17375
Or visit their web site: www.knouse.com

SAUSAGE RECIPES

Discover a ton of tasty new ways of enjoying sausages with the *Hillshire Farm Sausage recipes*. For your free copy send a postcard to:

HILLSHIRE FARMS
PO BOX 25111

CINCINNATI, **OH 45225**
You can also visit their web site:
www.hillshirefarm.com

DINNER PANCAKES

From the makers of Mrs. Butterworth's buttered
syrup, comes a nice collection of budget recipes that
will appeal to any palate. Send a postcard asking
for *"Mrs. Butterworth's Inflation Fighting Recipes"*
to:
LEVER BROTHERS CO.
390 PARK AVE.
NEW YORK, **NY 10022**

NOT FOR DIETERS

Here's a yummy collection of *Centennial Classics Recipes."* Selections
like Chocolate Peppermint
Whirlaway Pie will make your
mouth water just thinking about
it. Your diet can wait 'til next
month. Also ask for *A Profile Of
Hershey Foods.* Drop a card to:

HERSHEY'S KITCHEN
CONSUMER RELATIONS
100 CRYSTAL A DRIVE
PO BOX 815
HERSHEY, **PA 17033**
OR CALL: **1-800-468-1714**
Their web address is: www.hersheys.com

V.I.P. FROM IDAHO

Heart Healthy recipes will provide you with some
tasty recipe plus handy tips on buying and storing
Idaho Potatoes. Write to:
IDAHO POTATO COMMISSION
P.O. BOX 1068
BOISE, **ID 83701**

GEORGIA PEACH

Like peaches? You're gonna love Georgia Peach
Cobler, Peach Salsa, and other low fat recipes us-
ing peaches. Send a long SASE and ask for *Georgia
Classic and Timeless Peaches:*
GEORGIA DEPARTMENT OF AGRICULTURE

COMMODITIES PROMOTION
19 MARTIN LUTHER KING, JR. DRIVE SW
ATLANTA, GA 30334
Web address: www.agr.state.ga.us

DELICIOSA

If you are afraid to enjoy pasta meals just because you're on a diet— this one's for you. With *Super Solutions For Super Suppers* you'll enjoy delicious Italian meals that are nutritionally balanced and still allow you to lose weight. You'll also receive a discount coupon. Send to:
RAGU FOODS, INC.
33 BENEDICT PL.
GREENWICH. CT 06830

SPICE UP YOUR GRILL

Grey Poupon Dijon Mustard has a terrific book that features a host of different ways to spice up your menu with Grey Poupon Dijon Mustard. Here are tasty recipe ideas for red meat, chicken, pasta, fish and more. Ask for *Grill Recipes Using Dijon Mustard.* Visit them on the web at:
WWW.GREYPOUPON.COM

SWEET AS AN...ONION?

An onion is probably the last thing you think of when you think of sweet foods. Vidalia Onion would like to change your mind. These special onions are mild and tasty. They're grown only in a small section of Georgia where weather and soil conditions blend to make the World's Sweetest Onion. Send today for the Vidalia Onion recipe collection which will also show you how to freeze and store these unique onions. Send a SASE to:
VIDALIA SWEET ONIONS
P.O. BOX 1810
VIDALIA, GA 30474
1-800-892-3412
Also, check out their web site:
www.sweetvidalias.com

SEAFOOD DELIGHT

This compact collection of seafood recipe ideas comes to you from Lassco Smoked Salmon. You'll find tasty delights that'll make your next barbecue more fun, and gourmet delicacies to liven up any meal. When you write, ask for Seafood Recipes from Lassco." It's your free from:

LASSCO
778 KOHLER ST.
LOS ANGELES, CA 90021

BIRTHDAY PARTY PLANNER

Before you plan your child's next birthday party, be sure to send for this freebie. Skippy has put together some great party ideas from invitations to decorations and activities. Ask for *Skippy Peanut Butter Party Planner* from:

SKIPPY PEANUT BUTTER
DEPT. SPP, BOX 307
COVENTRY, CT 06238

BASKET OF FRESH IDEAS

This collection of strawberry recipes will show you how to use this tasty fruit to make mouth watering desserts and drinks. Send a card to:

CALIFORNIA STRAWBERRY ADVISORY BOARD
P.O. BOX 269
WATSONVILLE, CA 95077
Check out their web site: www.calstrawberry.com

BEES & HONEY

Here's a double-barreled special. Fascinating facts about bees and honey plus a collection of taste tempting recipes using golden honey. Just ask for *Cook It Right With Honey.* Send a postcard to:

DADANT & SONS
HAMILTON, IL 62341

TOP HITS FROM FRITO LAYS

This new recipe collection *Baked Low Fat - Taste The Fun Not The Fat* will provide you with a host of innovative new ways to enjoy Tostitos Tortilla Chips. Enjoy Chicken Curry Nachos or Italian Nachos. You'll also learn the story of Frito-Lay. It's yours

free from:
FRITO-LAY
PO Box 660634
DALLAS, TX 75266
1-800-352-4477
Visit their web site: www.fritolay.com

A TOUCH OF TABASCO

Add a little zest to your next meal with these recipes using Tabasco sauce. Send a card asking for *From The Land of Tabasco Sauce*. This cookbook features dozens of tangy and tasty meal ideas and recipes for everything from Holiday Turkey to Cream Onion Dip. Put a little spice in your life and your meals. Write to:
MCILHENNY CO.
AVERY ISLAND, LA 70513
www.tabasco.com

ADVENTURES IN GOOD EATING

Looking for new meal ideas your whole family will enjoy? Meals such as Stuffed Pork Chops and Tangy Chicken are among those you'll find in the *Heinz Recipe Collection*. Also ask for the *Heinz Cooking With Beans*. All free from:
H. J. HEINZ
PO Box 57
PITTSBURGH, PA 15230
Visit them on the web at: www.heinz.com

HOT STUFF

If you like your food red hot, you'll definitely want to send for this. *Tempting Recipes With Red Devil Hot Sauce* will show you some great ways to spice up your meals. You will also receive a Red Devil discount coupon and a Tabasco catalog. Send a card to:
B. F. TRAPPEY'S SONS. INC.
BOX 400
NEW IBERIA, LA 70560

YAM IT UP

How would you like to enjoy a marshmallow yam dessert or yam orange cookies? These are just two of the tasty treats you'll find featured in the *Sweet Potato recipe* collection with dozens of prize winning yam recipes. Free from:

LOUISIANA SWEET POTATO COMMISSION
P.O. BOX 2550
BATON ROUGE, LA 70821
WWW.SWEETPOTATO.ORG

COOKING WITH SWEET POTATOES

Here's a collection of over 70 tasty meals using sweet potatoes. You'll enjoy the main dishes and colorful casseroles featuring sweet potatoes in combination with other vegetables and meats. Visit the North Carolina Sweet Potato Commission on the web at:

www.ncsweetpotatoes.com

SHERRY, SHERRY

The makers of the original cream sherry – Harvey's Bristol Cream have a great recipe collection just for the asking. You'll find Peachy Cranberry Sauce for pork, Millionaire's Manhattan plus lots more. Send a long SASE and ask for *HBC's Recipes* to:

HBC RECIPE COLLECTION
PO BOX 767
HOLMDEL, NJ 07733
www.harveysbc.com

SALAD DRESSING

This small collection gives you 5 recipes using Uncle Dan's Salad Dressing and shows how it can be used as seasoning, for party dips and even as a sandwich spread. Write to:

UNCLE DAN'S
PO BOX 3325
SPOKANE, WA 99220
1-800-777-8874

For even more great recipes visit their web site at:
www.uncledans.com

COOKOUTS ARE FUN

The *Grill Lovers Catalog* has something every barbecue chef will enjoy having. It yours free from:
BRADLEY GRILL LOVER'S CATALOG
BOX 1300
COLUMBUS, GA 31902
1-800-241-7548

GARDEN OF EDEN

The fig has been with us ever since Adam and Eve decided that fig leaves made nifty apparel. Now *Buyers Guide To Dietary Fiber* along with *Fabulous Figs - The Fitness Fruit* and *This Fig Can Teach You A Lot About Nutrition* will give you delicious new ways to use this delightful and nutritious fruit. Free from:
FIG ADVISORY BOARD
3425 NORTH FIRST ST SUITE 109
FRESNO, CA 93726
1-800-588-2344
Or visit them on the web at:
www.californiafigs.com

UMMM ... GOOD

Campbell has a special collection of recipes along with a discount coupon waiting for you. They feature their tasty line of soups. When you write ask for the *Golden Corn Soup Chronology.* Write to:
CAMPBELL SOUP CO.
HOME ECONOMICS DEPT.
CAMPBELL PLACE
CAMDEN, NJ 08101
For over 1,500 great recipes go to their web site at:
www.campbellsoup.com

ALMOND SPECIALTIES

For a change of pace try using almonds to flavor your next meal. The *Fast & Fabulous* collection will show you how to use almonds in everything from chocolate-almond apricot bread, turkey tetrazzini almondine and almond-blueberry fruit cake. Free from:
ALMOND BOARD OF CALIFORNIA
12TH STREET, BOX 31307

MODESTO, CA 95354
For tons of great ideas and recipes, visit their web
site at:
www.almondsarein.com

TEXASWEET CITRUS RECIPES

This collection of mouth-watering citrus recipes comes to you from
TexaSweet. Their Ruby Red grapefruit
has a sweet, juicy flavor. The recipes
cover breakfast, dinner, dessert and
drinks using this delectable citrus.
Send a postcard to:
TEXASWEET CITRUS MARKETING
901 BUSINESS PARK DRIVE #100
MISSION. TX 78572
www.texasweet.com

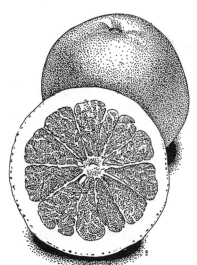

OLIVE OIL RECIPES

When dinner's done you may receive a standing ova-
tion from your family for the meal you just made
with the help of this recipe collection. *How To
Change Your Oil & Recipes* will give you a couple
of dozen creative meal ideas using olive oil. You will
also receive a store discount coupon. Send a card
to:
POMPEIAN INC.
DEPT. WS
PO BOX 8863
BALTIMORE, MD 21224
1-800-POMPEIAN
WWW.POMPEIAN.COM

SWEET 'N LOW SAMPLES

For an envelope full of Sweet 'N Low samples plus
a handy carry case, just send a SASE and request
Sweet 'N Low Samples. Send to:
SWEET 'N LOW
CUMBERLAND PACKING CORP
2 CUMBERLAND ST.
BROOKLYN, NY 11205
1-800-858-4200
For tons of recipes using Sweet 'N Low, visit them
on the web at:
www.sweetnlow.com

BUTTER IT UP

One call to the Best of Butter Hotline will reveal a world of ideas, recipes and tips on how to use Kellers Hotel Bar Butter in delighful new ways. When you call you will be taken step-by-step through the special recipe for that month. To find out more about their new recipes, cooking tips and product information, contact:

KELLER'S/HOTEL BAR FOODS
1-800-582-4382
For a great selection of tasty recipes, go to their web site at:
www.gourmetfood4u.com

FRESH FROM FLORIDA

What a wonderful package this is—an outstanding collection of recipes and information on seafood and aquaculture. Discover how to make a Seafare Saute & lots more. Send a long SASE to:

COMMISSIONER OF AGRICULTURE & CONSUMER SERVICES
BUREAU OF SEAFOOD & AQUACULTURE
2051 EAST DIRAC DR.
TALLAHASSEE, FL 32310
WWW.FL-SEAFOOD.COM

BE CREATIVE

The *Light & Elegant Cookbook* includes recipes of all kinds with everything from soups to nuts. All these exciting meals feature Lea & Perrins Sauce. There's even a nice index to help you easily find the recipe you want. Free from:

LEA & PERRINS SAUCE
CALL THEM AT: **1-800-987-4674**
Or visit them on the web at: www.lea-perrins.com

THOMAS' PROMISES..

If you like Thomas' English Muffins plain—you'll love 'em fancy. To get their *English Muffins Recipes* plus a discount coupon, call: S.B. Thomas, Inc. at:
1-800-356-3314

"NUTRITION FACTS"

Oscar Mayer sandwich spreads are easy and versatile to use. Try the spreads on crackers, breads

and in other recipes. For a nice collection of recipe ideas, send a postcard to:
OSCAR MAYER
DEPT. ST, P.O. BOX 7188
MADISON, WI 53707
www.oscarmayer.com

YOUNG AT HEART
If you are one of the 60 million Americans with high blood pressure, you should learn how to eat right. Send for the free booklet, *So You Have High Blood Cholesterol* from:
INFORMATION CENTER
NATIONAL HEART, LUNG, & BLOOD INSTITUTE
7200 WISCONSIN AVE.
PO BOX 30105
BETHESDA, MD 20824
Also check out their web site: www.nhlbi.nih.gov

NUTS ABOUT NUTS
If you're crazy about nuts, *All The Goodness of Hawaii is* the catalog for you. You can order anything from Macadamia Nuts to Kona Coffee. For your free copy, send a postcard to:
MAUNA LOA GIFT CENTER
1 MACADAMIA ROAD
H. C. 01, BOX 3
HILO, HI 96720
www.maunaloa.com

A SWEET WAY TO CHEAT
If you love sweets (and who doesn't) but must watch your weight *26 Ways To Get Back To Nature* is for you. For your free copy of this booklet plus four others including *Cakes For All Occasions*, send a postcard to:
SUGAR FOODS CORP.
9500 EL DORADO AVE.
SUN VALLEY CA 91353
IN CALIFORNIA CALL: 1-800-424-1919
OUTSIDE CALIFORNIA CALL: 1-800-732-8963

'YOU DON'T HAVE TO FRY IT TO LOVE IT'
If you're a catfish lover...this one's for you. These recipes are quick and easy to prepare. You'll dis-

cover many delicious (and healthy) ways of preparing catfish without frying it. To get your catfish recipe collection, write to:

THE CATFISH INSTITUTE
BOX 247
118 HAYDEN ST.
BELZONI, MS 39038

For even faster delivery of this free collection call them toll-free at:

1-800-877-4321

Or visit them online at: www.catfishinstitute.com

CREOLE COOKING

If you enjoy the unique taste and flavors of cajon and creole food, this one's for you. For a free copy of chef Paul Prudhomme's Magic Spice Book showing you how to use creole seasoning to create old-fashioned Louisiana taste delights. Call toll-free:

1-800-457-2857

www.chefpaul.com

EIGHT FOR DINNER

The American Lamb Council several recipe collections that will show you exciting ways to make your dinners more delightful. The collection includes *Make It Simple, Make It Sizzle,* and *Festive Lamb Recipes,* plus several others. You'll find wine-basted, marinated, grilled, roasted and broiled recipes using fresh American lamb. Send a long SASE to:

THE AMERICAN LAMB COUNCIL
6911 S. YOSEMITE ST. SUITE 200
ENGLEWOOD, CO 80112
Visit their web site at: www.lambchef.com

BRING HOME THE BACON

If you like bacon, be sure to get your copy of *Savor The Flavor, Round The Clock With Oscar Mayer Bacon.* In it you'll discover tasty recipes and cooking ideas featuring bacon. They will also include party & cookout recipes using Oscar Mayers Little Wieners & Little Smokies plus Nutrition Facts. Send a postcard to:

BACON BOOKLET
OSCAR MAYER CONSUMER CENTER
PO BOX 7188
MADISON, WI 53707
www.oscarmayer.com

DELICIOUS SKINNY BEEF

Looking for something easy but delicious for your family's meals? How about meals that are perfect for anyone watching their weight? Try something different... like 'beef, pasta & artichoke toss' or 'quick steak & vegetable soup'. For some great recipes visit the Meat Board Test Kitchens on the internet at:

www.beef.org (then click on 'kitchen')

HOW TO COMFORT

Now you can make some great desserts, drinks even coffee using that versatile liquor from Kentucky — Southern Comfort. If you want more delicious recipe ideas, write:

**SOUTHERN COMFORT COMPANY
DEPT. GT, BOX 1080
LOUISVILLE, KY 40201**

WINE AND DINE

The Gallo recipe collection will provide you with dozens of palate pleasing ways of using Gallo to enhance your next meal. Included is a delightful recipe for Goumet Pizza and lots more. These recipes will let you turn everyday cooking into an adventure. Write to:

**E & J GALLO WINERY
MODESTO, CA 95353**

"WHITE WINE RECIPES"

Wine lovers delight in trying new wines and new ways to enjoy familiar wines. With this compact collection of recipes you'll create tasty new meals using the fine wines of Widmer. Free from:

**WIDMER WINE CELLARS
116 BUFFALO ST.
CANANDAIGUA, NY 14424
1-800-836-5253
WWW.WIDMERWINE.COM**

WINE LOVERS

"Beaulieu Vineyards" describes and pictures the Beaulieu line of fine wines. Also includes a card for a free

wine tasting tour of their vineyard. Write to:
BEAULIEU VINEYARDS
PO BOX 329
RUTHERFORD, CA 94573

CORDIAL RECIPES

Hiram Walker has put together a selection of over 30 famous food and drink recipes from around the world. These recipes all feature their fine line of cordials. Just ask for their free *The Best Of Kahlua*. Pink Chinchilla Pie anyone? Write to:
ALLIED DOMECQ
KAHLUA BRAND MANAGER
355 RIVERSIDE AVE.
WESTPORT, CT 06880
www.allieddomecqplc.com

CHAMBORD RECIPES

Chambord is a liqueur made with small black raspberries plus other fruits & herbs combined with honey. For new ways to enjoy this magnificent liqueur, send for the free *Chambord Recipe Book* from:
CHAMBORD RECIPES
2633 TRENTON AVE
PHILADELPHIA, PA 19125
1-800-523-3811

VIRGIN ISLAND RUM

Cruzan Rum is an exceptionally clean tasting rum that works well with mixers or on its own. For your copy of the free *Imported Rum Recipes,* visit them on the web at:
www.cruzanrums.com

A TOUCH OF MEXICO FROM YOUR COMPUTER

If you're looking for a tasty change in your usual dinner fare, why not try a novel Mexican meal. It's called *Mexican Meals Made Easy* and it's brought to you by the folks at Ortega. At their web site you will find interesting recipes for Mexican dinners using just the ingredients you have on hand. Visit them at their web site:
www.ortegafoods.com

WHAT'S IN YOUR CUPBOARD?

If you have a computer, Uncle Ben's has a terrific idea to help you make a quick and simple dinners using just the ingredients you have on hand. When you visit their web site you'll have over 1,000 recipes from Uncle Ben's kitchen right at your fingertips. Simply input the ingredients you have in your cupboard and they'll supply you with a delicious dish you can whip up in no time. This unique cooking site also offers helpful shopping lists, product information, healthy lifestyle tips and more. Visit their web site at:
www.unclebens.com

MORE COOKING HELP
VIA THE INTERNET

Here are three sites you can visit for cooking help, tips and ideas:

BETTER HOMES AND GARDENS

At this site you'll find loads of interesting ideas for all areas of your home...menu plans, cooking tips, crafts, parties and gardening. You'll also find a helpful cold, flu and allergy guide and even interesting decorating ideas. Check it out at:
www.bhglive.com

EPICURIOUS

Here you'll find tips, theme menu ideas, vegetarian recipes as well as beer and wine suggestions. Visit them at:
www.epicurious.com

COOKING.COM

If you've looking for interesting traditional and alternative menu ideas and products, you must visit this Internet site at:
www.cooking.com

For Home & Garden

POTPOURRI BONNETS

These delightful miniature straw hat bonnet magnets are filled with potpourri and ready for your refrigerator or bath room. They are yours for two first class loose stamps. Send to:
VALERIE'S HATTERY
13435 S. CEDAR RD
CEDAR, MI 49621

WORRY-FREE: SEPTIC SYSTEM

If you have a septic system, time may be running out before your system fails. Before that happens, the makers of RID-X would like to send you this informative booklet, which can help you avoid septic system failure. Send a card to:
RID-X
DEPT. MBD
MONTVALE, NJ 07645

SOLAR ENERGY & YOUR HOME

One day your home may be heated and powered with free energy from the sun. Here are the answers to many of the most frequently asked questions about putting solar and other kinds of renewable energy to work for you. Write to:
EREC
EE90
1000 INDEPENDENCE AVE. SW
WASHINGTON, DC 20585

There is a toll-free phone number you can call to get in touch directly with an expert who can answer specific questions you may have about renewable energy. There are also a large number of free booklets dealing with all aspects of renewable energy available by calling the same 800 number.
CALL: 1-800-363-3732

Finally, if you have a computer, you can access the Energy Efficiency & Renewable Energy Clearinghouse run by the Department of Energy, on the Internet. They even have free software you can download. Their web site is located at:
www.eren.doe.gov

"TIPS FOR ENERGY SAVERS"

Saving energy not only makes America less energy dependent on other nations - it will save you a tidy sum of money too. The Department of Energy would like you to have a useful energy-saving package. Ask for the *"Energy Saver Booklets."* It's yours free from:
D.O.E. TECHNICAL INFORMATION CENTER
BOX 62
OAK RIDGE, TN 37830
www.osti.gov

WHAT DOES FIBERGLAS DO?

All About Insulation and *Owens-Corning Fiberglas* are two of the useful guides found in the "Fiberglas information series". You'll find out how Fiberglas is made and how it's used for insulation, dust-stops and air filters. Free from:
OWENS CORNING
ONE OWENS CORNING PKWY
TOLEDO, OH 43659
1-800-438-7465
www.owenscorning.com

HOME REMODELING IDEAS

Are you getting ready to build or remodel? The *Insider's Look At Building Your Home* and *Insider's Look At Remodeling Your Home* are an absolute must. Your creative juices will begin to flow as you thumb through these beautifully illustrated idea books. The answer books will provide help in solving your remodeling problems whether adding a room or simply changing a window. Write to:
ANDERSEN CORP.
BAYPORT, MN 55003
1-800-426-4261 EXT **2837**
Their web address is: **www.andersenwindows.com**

IN-SINK ERATOR

If you're considering a garbage disposal, trash compactor or hot water dispenser check out In-Sink Erator. Ask for their *information package* and then decide which is best for your needs and budget. Write:

IN-SINK ERATOR
4700 21ST ST.
RACINE, WI 53406

LET THE SUN SHINE IN

If you're planning on building or remodeling a house, have you thought about which windows and doors are right for you? *Window Scaping* tells all about the many types of windows and doors available to help you to decide for yourself. It's free from:

PELLA CO.
102 MAIN STREET
PELLA, IA 50219
1-888-84-PELLA
www.pella.com

STAIN REMOVAL

This helpful *Emergency Spot Removal Guide* will help you get rid of some of the trickiest stains you may get on your carpets or draperies. It is free for the asking and will come with discount coupons. Drop a postcard to:

COIT DRAPERY & CARPET CLEANERS
DEPT. ABJ, 897 HINKLEY RD.
BURLINGAME, CA 94010

FREE SAMPLES OF STAIN

If you are planning on staining any wood in, on or around your home, one of the finest products you can use is Cabot Stains. But often it is difficult to tell just what a particular color stain will look like before you actually put it on your wood and try it out. To get sample cans of up to 4 different color stains, first get a color chart from a paint store and select the colors you would like to try. Then   call

Cabot's Consumer Hotline and request free sample cans and a paint brush. Call them toll-free at:
1-800-US-STAINS

BEAUTIFY & PROTECT YOUR HOME

Red Devil would like to show you the right way to beautify your home with wall coverings and protect it with caulk. Ask them for the free *wallcovering and caulk booklets.* Write to:
**RED DEVIL INC.
CONSUMER RELATIONS
PO BOX 3133
UNION, NJ 07083**

WALLPAPER BY MAIL

This great *catalog* offers you an excellent selection of high quality wall covering products at low prices. To make your selection easier, they will send you free swatches of the paper and even matching fabrics. Send a postcard to:
**ROBINSON'S WALLCOVERINGS
225 WEST SPRING ST.
TITUSVILLE, PA 16354**

"STORY OF HARDWOOD PLYWOOD"

If you are a handyman you will enjoy this informative booklet which gives the whole story of plywood. Best of all you'll receive a set of 4 different plans showing you how to build a bookcase, room divider, saddle seat desk and TV trays (planter/desk/stereo, etc.) All free from:
**HARDWOOD PLYWOOD MANUFACTURERS
PO BOX 2789
RESTON, VA 22090**

GUIDE TO PAINT & VARNISH REMOVAL

In this handy guide you will learn some great and easy ways to improve the appearance of your house. There are quick and easy methods for removing mildew and mildew stains from both interior and exterior surfaces. These helpful hints are a must for any tough cleaning job. Send for your free guide to:

SAVOGRAN COMPANY
P.O. Box 130
NORWOOD, MA 02062
1-800-225-9872
www.savogran.com

BUILDING A HOUSE

Even though the prices of homes have skyrocked, you may still be able to afford the home you've always wanted. For the past quarter century DeGeorge Homes has helped over 15,000 people enjoy home ownership with their step-by-step instructions and pre-cut materials. For a free copy of their 80 page *color catalog* with 50 exciting models to choose from, write to:

DEGEORGE HOMES
55 REALTY DRIVE
CHESHIRE, CT 06410
OR CALL THEM AT: 1-800-342-7576

"SAVE WATER"

Here's a fully illustrated guide on how to pinpoint water waste in your toilet and what to do about it. You'll also receive a sample of the dye used to detect leaks. Drop a postcard to:

FLUIDMASTER
30800 RANCHO VIEJO ROAD
SAN JUAN CAPISTRANO, CA 92675
1-800-631-2011
www.fluidmaster.com

AMGARD SECURITY

To protect your family and home, a home security alarm system is essential. To help you decide on what type of protection is best for you and your family ask for the free *Amgard Security Planning Guide.* Drop a card to:

AMGARD SECURITY OFFER
AMWAY CORPORATION-33A-2J
ADA, MI 49355

THE ALL PURPOSE WONDER

Want to save money and look good too? Send for *This Little Box With A House Full of Uses.* In it you will learn how to use baking soda in ways you never thought of...in the kitchen, bathroom, basement, even on your pet. Write to:

ARM & HAMMER
CONSUMER RELATIONS
CHURCH & DWIGHT CO.
PRINCETON, NJ 08543
1-800-524-1328
www.armhammer.com

STAIN REMOVAL

Most stains can be removed by following certain procedures. The people at Maytag have an excellent stain removal guide they will send to you just for the asking. Remember, once you master the steps it's easy to remove just about any stain by referring to this handy guide. You'll also receive *Facts of Laundry.- Choosing The Right Laundry Additives.* Send a postcard to:

MAYTAG COMPANY
CUSTOMER SERVICE
240 EDWARDS STREET
CLEVELAND, TN 37311
1-800-688-9900
www.maytag.com

CARPET CLEANING

Hoover will send you a free guide to carpet care. The *Consumer Guide to Carpet Cleaning* is loaded with carpet care tips and facts, cleaning alternatives , a stain removal chart and more. This 16 page booklet provides important information you should know. Ask for *Consumer Guide to Carpet Cleaning. Send a* SASE to:

THE HOOVER COMPANY
CONSUMER EDUCATION, DEPT. FC
101 E. MAPLE ST.
NORTH CANTON, OH 44720

SHINGLE IT

Lots of remodeling ideas are contained in this great *Red Shingle & Shake package.* It shows how to use

shingles and shakes outside and inside your house. These guides also show how to do-it-yourself and save. Drop a card to:
CEDAR SHAKE & SHINGLE BUREAU
PO BOX 1178
SUMAS, WA 98295
www.cedarbureau.org

COLORS & CLOROX

Here are lots of helpful tips from Clorox on keeping your clothes clean, bright and stain free. Ask for *Emergency Spot Removal Guide*. Drop a card to:
THE CLOROX CO.
1221 BROADWAY
OAKLAND, CA 94612
1-800-292-2200
www.clorox.com

GLISTENING SILVER

If you would like to keep your silverware shining like new, try storing it in Hagerty's Tarnish Intercept Bags. Once the silverware is placed inside and the bag zipper is closed, it locks out tarnish. The inside of the bag will blacken when it has absorbed all the corrosion-causing gases. You then remove the silver and place it in a new bag. For information on their line of precious metal care products, call: **1-800-348-5162** x103
W. J. HAGERTY SONS, LTD.
P.O. BOX 1496
SOUTH BEND, IN 46624.
OR VISIT THEIR WEB SITE: www.hagerty-polish.com

STAIN OUT HOTLINE

Do you have questions about problem stains on those favorite garments What do you do if it's an unknown mystery stain and you don't know where to begin? The Dow Stain Experts, the makers of Spray'N Wash, have the answers for you. Give them a call at:
1-800 260-1066

CHOOSING CARPETING

Dupont Company offers you this free booklet *"Consumer's Guide To Choosing Carpets"* to help answer all your questions about carpet care. Drop

a card to:
Dupont Co.
Room G 40284
Wilmington, DE 19898.

LIGHT UP YOUR GARDEN

Like to add a colorful look to your garden? Consider using Holland or domestic bulbs. For a full color catalog write to:

Van Bourgondien
PO 1000
Babylon, NY 11702
1-800-622-9997
www.dutchbulbs.com

BURPEE GARDENS

This catalog is packed with everything you can imagine to start your vegetable, flower or fruit garden. They have seed starter kits and plants. You'll even find garden helpers, bird houses and fun seed kits for kids. Grow your own herb garden right on your kitchen window sill. When you call or write mention OFFER #82 and in addition to their new *Flowering Bulb and Perennial Catalogue*, you'll also receive a special $5.00-off coupon. Free from:

Burpee & Co.
300 Park Ave
Warminster, PA 18974
or call 1-800-888-1447
www.burpee.com

WHY PLANTS FAIL

The question of why some plants fail to grow even when they are carefully tended to, has always been somewhat of a mystery. Now Gurney Seed and Nursery would like to throw some light on the subject so you can have a more beautiful garden. They will also send you the new *Gurney Catalog*. It features over 4000 items—many shown in full color. You'll find how-to-grow-it tips plus planting charts and moisture guides along with many special offers. If you'd like a packet of giant sunflower seeds, include a quarter. Write:

Gurney's Seed & Nursery Co.

110 CAPITAL STREET
YANKTON SD 57079
WWW.GURNEYS.COM

GO ORGANIC

How To Grow An Organic Garden will get you started raising your own delicious and naturally pure vegetables. It even includes a plan for a sample garden. Get your free copy and let Mother Nature do her thing. Write to:

ORGANIC GARDENING & FARMING
33 E. MINOR ST.
EMMAUS, PA 18049

GROWING IDEAS

In the last few years backyard community gardens have been popping up all over the nation. Bring your community together and save money too - start a community garden. You'll also receive teaching tools to help young minds grow. Ask for the free *Growing Ideas package* from:

NATIONAL GARDEN ASSOCIATION
180 FLYNN AVE.
BURLINGTON, VT 05401

EXOTIC IMPORTED PLANTS

If you enjoy unusual and out-of-the ordinary type plants this one's for you. The new *Stokes seed catalog* features 1300 varieties including many imported from England, Europe, and Canada. Get your free catalog from:

STOKES SEEDS
BOX 548
BUFFALO, NY 14240
1-800-396-9238
WWW.STOKESEEDS.COM

MILLER'S NURSERY GUIDE

In this new catalog you'll find a new seedless grape, virus-free berries and several pages of tested recipes and a whole lot more. Miller Nurseries has put together a broad selection of their most popular nursery items. Ask for their new *Catalog & Planting Guide*:

J. E. MILLER NURSERIES
5060 WEST LAKE ROAD
CANANDAIGUA, NY 14424
1-800-836-9630
WWW.MILLERNURSERIES.COM

LAWN CARE

Here's a super 5-star special for anyone with a lawn or garden. To help improve lawn, flowers, vegetable garden, trees and shrubs - call the experts at Scott Lawn Products on their toll-free phone. They have the answers to any and all questions about lawn growing, disease, fertilizing, problem areas etc. They'll give you a free subscription to *"Lawn Care"* with loads of useful information (plus money saving coupons). They'll be happy to send you any of the dozens of booklets, magazines and brochures that will help you grow the perfect lawn or garden. Excellent. Call toll free:

1-800-543-8873 OR WRITE:
SCOTT LAWN PRODUCTS
14111 SCOTTS LAWN RD.
MARYVILLE, OH 43041
Or visit their web site: www.scottscompany.com

FREE FERTILIZER

Free manure is available to gardeners through Extension Services located throughout the country. To find the one nearest you, call your local U.S. Department of Agriculture Extension Service. You'll find their number in your local phone book.

GREAT GARDENS

The Burreil Seed Growers have a nice seed catalog every home gardener will want to have. Before you get ready to plant your next garden be sure to get a copy of this catalog. Send a postcard to:

D.V. BURREIL SEED
GROWERS CO.
PO BOX 150
ROCKY FORD, CO 81067

GARDENER'S HANDBOOK

If you want to learn how to have a beautiful fruitful garden, be sure to get a free copy of *The Park Gardener's Handbook.* In it you will find all kinds of useful information that will help you to get more productive results from your gardening efforts. You can also choose from over 3000 new and rare varieties of flowers and vegetables as well as the more familiar types—all available from the full color Park catalog you'll receive. To get yours send a postcard to:

PARK SEED CO.
1 PARKTON AVE.
GREENWOOD, SC 29649
1-800-213-0076
www.parkseed.com

FULL-SIZE FRUIT FROM DWARF-SIZE TREES

If your yard is too small to grow as many fruit trees as you'd like, take a look at this free catalog. These dwarf trees grow only 8 to 10 feet tall but grow full size apples, peaches, pears, cherries, and nectarines. This catalog features almost 400 varieties of fruit, shade and nut trees plus shrubs, vines, ornamentals, and award-winning roses. Send a postcard for the catalog and special offers to:

STARK BROTHER NURSERIES
BOX 1800, HIGHWAY 54W
LUISIANA, MO 63353
1-800-775-6415
WWW.STARKBROTHERS.COM

Staying Healthy

FREE HEADACHE RELIEF

We all live in a fast-paced, stress-full society and trying to balance work, family and social life can take its toll. If you suffer from stress related headaches, the folks at Excedrin would like to help. First, there's their free colorful newsletter, *Excedrin Headache Relief Update.* You'll learn the warning signs and some common foods that trigger migraines. There's also a readers corner where experts answer your questions. You'll even receive a coupon towards your next purchase of Excedrin. They also have a toll-free customer service number you can call for help and an excellent web site. For help with your persistent headache problems, contact them at:

EXCEDRIN HEADACHE RESOURCE CENTER
PO BOX 687
WILTON, CT 06897
Or call them toll-free at:
1-800-468-7746
You can also visit their web site at:
www.excedrin.com

HEALTHY, HAPPY KIDS

If you're a parent or about to become one, here are three free publications you will want to get:

Sneak Health Into Your Snacks put out by the American Institute For Cancer Research, will show you how to get your kids to eat healthy meals without them knowing that it's good for them. For your free copy, send a long SASE to:
AICR
1759 R STREET NW

Washington, DC 20009
Or better yet, call them toll-free at:
1-800-843-8114

Especially For Teens: You And Your Sexuality is a free brochure that will help your teens better understand and deal with their budding sexuality. To get a copy, send a long SASE requesting publication # APO42 to:
**ACOG Resource Center
PO Box 96920
Washington, DC 20090**

Your Child And Antibiotics will tell you more about the important role antibiotics can play in keeping your child healthy. To get your free copy, send a long SASE to:
**American Academy of Pediatrics
Publications Division
141 Northwest Point Blvd.
PO Box 747
Elk Grove Village, IL 60009**

CHILD SAFETY
Hidden Hazards II spotlights potential family safety risks. Every parent is interested in the safety of their child and the products that are around that are safe and hazardous. Ask for *Hidden Hazards II*. For your free copy, send a SASE to:
**Coalition for Consumer Health and Safety
PO Box 12099
Washington, DC 20005-0999**

BREAST FEEDING GUIDE
If you are a new mother or soon to be one, this handy *Breast Feeding Guide* will answer most of the questions you may have about breast feeding. Write for this excellent information to:
**Medela, Inc.
PO Box 660
Mc Henry, IL 60051-0660**

HAVING A BABY?

If you are about to have a baby or if you've recently had a newborn, this one's for you. It's called *The Mayo Clinic Complete Book of Pregnancy & Baby's First Year* and it's yours free from the 'good neighbor' folks at State Farm. This beautiful 750 page book covers all aspects of pregnancy and baby care through age one. It is not only one of the most comprehensive guides to baby care but also an excellent resource book you'll use over and over again. The book is divided into 4 sections...pregnancy, childbirth, living and understanding your baby and there's even a section 'from partners to parents: a family is born.' This beautiful book is a must for anyone starting a family. It also makes an excellent gift. To get your copy, contact your local State Farm Insurance agent or call them toll free at: **1-888-733-8368**

CHOLESTEROL & BLOOD PRESSURE

Call the National Heart, Lung and Blood Institute for recorded information on cholesterol and high blood pressure. When you call leave your name and address for written information. Call: **1-800-575-WELL**
OR VISIT THEM ON THE INTERNET: WWW.NHLBI.NIH.GOV

YOUNG AT HEART

The National Institute on Aging would like you to have a copy of *"For Hearts and Arteries: What Scientists are Learning About Age and the Cardiovascular System."* Learn how the latest research can help keep your heart running younger no matter what your age.
NIA INFORMATION CENTER
PO Box 8057
GAITHERSBURG, MD. **20898-8057**
OR CALL **1-800-222-2225**
WWW.NIH.GOV/NIA

NEW HOPE FOR ARTHRITIS SUFFERERS

The new millennium has brought about a host of new medicines for arthritis sufferers. To provide you with a one-stop source for all you need to know about these medications, the Arthritis Foundation has a free *Drug Guide* waiting for you. You'll find a list of hundreds of prescription and over-the-counter drugs commonly used for arthritis including information on various side effects, cautions and contraindications plus a special drug dosage diary. To get your copy, call them toll-free at:

1-800-283-7800
Or visit their web site at: www.arthritis.org

FREE LUNG DISEASE GUIDE

If you or someone you know has a lung disease, one essential guide you will want to get is a free copy of the *Lung Disease Resource Guide*. In it is a wealth of helpful information, resources and contacts including video tapes, books, organizations and toll-free health lines...even a glossary of terms. To get your free copy, call:

1-800-LUNG-USA (THAT'S 800-586-4872)
WWW.LUNGUSA.COM

NEWS ON NAILS

Healthy nails are gorgeous nails. But if you've noticed that your nails are discolored or getting thick or brittle, you may have what millions of people have – fungus-ridden nails. Fortunately there is something you can do. The first step should be to get the free brochure and video called *Barefoot Without Embarrassment: Uncovering The Inside Story On Nail Fungus*. Write to:

NOVARTIS PHARMACEUTICALS
PO Box 29201
SHAWNEE MISSION, KS 66201-9669

FREE HELP WITH SKIN PROBLEMS

If you suffer from red, itchy, scaling skin, you owe it to yourself to get help. Now there's a toll-free number you can call. It's called the *Exorex National Psoriasis and Eczema Helpline*. To help you achieve and sustain long-lasting remission, when you call you'll receive a mail-in rebate & coupon book providing you with savings on Exorex products. Call:

1-888-551-6300

STOP THAT ITCH

If you're bothered by an itching problem that is linked to hot weather, the makers of Lanacane have prepared a helpful brochure called, *A Guide To Summer Itching* you'll want to get. For your free copy, write to:

LANACANE ITCH INFORMATION CENTER
PO Box 328-LC
WHITE PLAINS, NY 10602

Or you can visit their web site at:
www.lanacane.com

THE MEN'S MAINTENANCE MANUAL

Did you know that women go to the doctor almost three times as often as men? Did you also know that women on average live 7 years longer than men? A recent survey showed that a huge percentage of men have not been to the doctor in years. That means that many diseases that could be prevented if caught early enough will go undetected in men until it's too late. To educate people about preventable disease, the National Men's Health Foundation has a free copy of *Men's Maintenance Manual*, a guide with advice on diet, stress and health risks plus a list of resources. To get your free copy, call:

1-800-955-2002

Or visit their web site at:
www.menshealth.com

DISCOVER THE WORLD OF NATURAL MEDICINE

If you are interested in learning about natural remedies and natural products and their effect on your body send for this *catalog of homeopathic remedies*. Enzymatic Therapy and Leaning offer you some of their natural methods of feeling better. They will even send you a $3.00 coupon to try Herpilyn, a cold sore remedy. To get answers to your questions, you can call their consumer information line.

1-800-783-2286

TENSION & DEPRESSION

The National Mental Health Association has lots of information on how to handle tension and depression. If you have any questions, they have a toll- free number and will send you helpful information. Call:

THE NATIONAL MENTAL HEALTH ASSOCIATION,
ALEXANDRIA, VA
1-800-969-6642

TEEN SMOKING

Centers for Disease Control's Offices on Smoking and Health will help you tackle questions on how to curb teen smoking. If you have a teenager and would like some specific advice, call:
1-800-CDC-1311

KEEPING YOUR HEART HEALTHY

The American Heart Association would like to help you take care of your heart. When you call their toll-free helpline, your call will be routed to your local AHA office for information on heart disease, strokes, high blood pressure and diet. Some offices can tell you about local support groups or low-cost or free screenings for blood pressure and cholesterol.

You can also get free copies of a variety of booklets dealing with your heart. Topics include blood pressure, CPR, cholesterol, diet, exercise, heart disease and strokes to mention just a few. Learn the best ways to eat smart and healthy by reducing fat in your diet. You'll also learn how to read the new food labels to help you shop for healthier foods. Ask for *Shop Smart With Heart* and *Eating Plan For Healthy Americans* and other heart-related topics you may be interested in. Write to:

THE AMERICAN HEART ASSOCIATION
NATIONAL CENTER
7272 GREENVILLE AVE.
DALLAS, TX **75231**
OR CALL: **1-800-AHA-USA-1** (that's 1-800-242-8721)
WWW.AMERICANHEART.ORG

SLEEP HOTLINE

The American Society of Travel Agents and Searle Provide tips on how to feel your best while traveling. Request a free brochure titled *Sleep Well... Stay Fit - Tips for Travelers."*
1-800-SHUTEYE
www.astanet.com

JOINT REPLACEMENT

If you or anyone you know ever needs joint replacement you will want to read this valuable information. You will learn Why and when it is necessary... how it is performed.. benefits...risks. Ask for *Total Joint Replacement.* Send a SASE to:
AMERICAN ACADEMY OF ORTHOPEDIC SURGEONS
6300 NORTH RIVER ROAD
ROSEMONT, IL 60018
1-800-346-AAOS
www.aaos.org

DO YOU HAVE BLADDER PROBLEMS?

Did you know that nearly half a milliom people suffer from interstitial cystitis an often misdiagnosed chronic bladder disorder. The National Institutes of Health has published a free booklet that gives basic information in layman's terms on the disease. Ask for *Interstitial Cystitis* by writing to:
IC BOOKLET
NATIONAL INSTITUTE OF DIABETES & DIGESTIVE & KIDNEY DISEASES
3 INFORMATION WAY
BETHESDA, MD. 20892-3580
www.niddk.nih.gov/health/health.htm

THE FACTS ABOUT PROSTATE CANCER

Early Detection of Prostate Cancer answers the most often -asked questions about prostate cancer. Although the disease is of prime concern to men over 55, it explains that the disease can often exist without symptoms and that men over 40 should tested annually. The National Cancer Institute also includes a list of problems that might indicate prostate cancer. It also covers the specifics of diagnosis, treatment, and prognosis- which is excellent if

the condition is caught early enough. For your free copy or to speak with a specialist call:
1-800-422-6237
WWW.NIDDK.NIH.GOV

CANCER HOTLINE

The National Cancer Institute's Information Service provides the latest information about cancer, including causes and medical referral to low-cost clinics, medical consultation, referral to patient support groups and publications on request. They can provide you with literature and answer questions concerning various types of cancer and the standard treatment. Send a card to:

NATIONAL CANCER INSTITUTE
31 CENTER DRIVE
MSC 2580 BUILDING 31 ROOM 10A31
BEETHESDA, MD 20892
OR CALL **1-800-4-CANCER**

A HEALTHIER YOU

Research shows that eating fresh fruits and vegetables help put more fiber in your diet and helps make for a healthier you. Information about the vitamins, minerals and fiber in fruits and vegetables are essential to a healthier you. This booklet from the American Institute for Cancer Research includes healthy recipes. Just send a SASE to:

THE AMERICAN INSTITUTE FOR CANCER RESEARCH
DEPT. AP
WASHINGTON, DC 20069

BACK TROUBLES?

The BackSaver catalog has a wonderful assortment of all types of products for your back, including chairs, seat and back support cushions, sleeping supports, reading tables and more. It's free from:

BACKSAVER PRODUCTS CO.
53 JEFFREY AVE.
HOLLISTON, MA 01746

NOW HEAR THIS

If you are experiencing hearing loss and your doctor has recommended a hearing aid, you may need help in determining what kind of device you need. The American Speech -Language-Hearing Associa-

tion, offers general information about hearing aids and their costs, insurance coverage, proper fit and care. For your free copy of *How to Buy a Hearing Aid* call:
1-800-638-8255

PARENT RESOURCE GUIDE

It's important for children to develop good eating habits when they are young so that they can grow up to be healthier, more active adults. The American Academy of Pediatrics has some important nutrition information just for the asking. Send a business sized SASE to:
NUTRITION BROCHURES DEPT. C
AMERICAN ACADEMY OF PEDIATRICS
141 NW POINT BLVD.
ELK GROVE VILLAGE, IL 60007
www.aap.org

ALLERGIES AND ASTHMA

If you have questions about allergies or asthma, here's how you can find answers. The Asthma and Allergy Foundation will answer any questions you have regarding the symptoms of allergies to different substances, foods and how all these can be related to asthma.
CALL: **1-800-7-ASTHMA** (THAT'S 800-727-8462)
www.aafa.org

ABC'S OF EYECARE

The Better Vision Institute has some worthwhile information on your eyes and how to take the best care of them. Topics include everything from the

proper selection of eyeglass frames, to eye care for children & adults, tips on correct lighting, correct type of sunglasses and more. Send a business-sized SASE to:
BETTER VISION INSTITUTE
1700 DIAGONAL ROAD
SUITE 500

ALEXANDRIA, VA 22314
OR CALL 1-800-424-8422
www.visionsite.org

DEPRESSION AWARENESS

Today we are very aware of everything around us and yet we sometimes blot out or deny the signs of depression in ourselves and those around us. This very informative information on depression is published by the National Institute of Mental Health. Learn all the facts and become aware. Send a business-sized, SASE to:
NIMH PUBLIC INQUIRY
6001 EXECUTIVE BLVD.
ROOM 8184 MSC 9663
BETHESDA, MD 20892
OR CALL: 1-800-421-4211
www.nimh.nih.gov

HEALTHY TEETH

Teeth: we get one set of permanent healthy adult teeth so it's essential to learn how to keep them strong and cavity free. Dental care is also a very important career opportunity that also allows you to help others take care of their teeth. If you think you may be interested in finding out more about career options, ask for a copy of *Dental Hygiene - A Profession of Opportunities* and also *Facts About Dental Hygiene*. Send a SASE to:
AMERICAN DENTAL HYGIENISTS' ASSOCIATION
444 N. MICHIGAN AVE.
CHICAGO, IL 60611
www.adha.org

PARALIMINAL TAPES

If you find it hard to learn new things, check our the 'Paraliminal Tapes'. Using this unique method of confusing the brain by providing different messages for the right brain and the left brain, reportedly can help you either learn a subject you are interested in or rapidly achieve a goal you've set for yourself. There are 22 unique paraliminal tapes. To learn more about whether this unique technique can help you, call for your free catalog today:
1-800-735-TAPE

HYSTERECTOMY - DO YOU REALLY NEED IT?

The American College of Obstetricians and Gynecologists has published a free pamphlet *Understanding Hysterectomy* which outlines what constitutes a medically necessary hysterectomy and describes what the surgery involves. Request a copy, it's free. Write:

ACOG
409 12TH ST. SW
WASHINGTON, DC 20090
WWW.ACOG.COM

HIKING SAFETY

Whether you are walking to lose weight, exploring a tourist attraction, or hiking to enjoy scenic trails, there are a number of guideline your should follow. Send a SASE and ask for *"Hiking Safety"* from:

AMERICAN HIKING SOCIETY
1422 FENWICK LANE
SILVER SPRING,, MD 20910
www.americanhiking.org

MASSAGE THERAPY

Stress got you down? The *Massage Therapy* booklet will give you detailed information about different methods of massage and benefits of each. It will also answer some of your questions. Write:

AMERICAN MASSAGE THERAPY ASSOCIATION
820 DAVIS ST., SUITE 100
EVANSTON, IL 60201
www.amtamassage.org

ASTHMA RELIEF

Asthma patients who use inhalers may be masking the physical cause for their symptoms. Doctors have come up with a checklist for asthma patients who rely on those inhalers to open their airways. If you use the inhaler more than three times a week, if you go through more than one canister a month, and if your asthma awakens you at night, you may be suffering from an inflammation of the airways that is the real cause of your symptoms and may need drug treatment to clear it up. To receive a free copy of the list, write to:

ASTHMA INFORMATION CENTER
BOX 790
SPRINGHOUSE, **PA 19477**

FREE CHILD'S HEALTH RECORD

This easy to use health record log is great for parents and kids alike. Keep your child's vital health records in this handy easy-to-read log. With it you will keep track of illnesses, allergies, health exams, immunizations and tests, family history and health insurance, It features the ever popular peanuts gang (Charlie Brown, Snoopy and friends) and is sure to be popular with the little ones. Ask for *Your Child's Health Record*. Call:
1-800-MET-LIFE

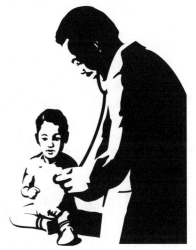

NUTRITION HOTLINE

Find out how your diet is affecting your health. Call the American Institute for Cancer Research, Nutrition Hotline and ask a registered dietician your personal questions on diet, nutrition and cancer. When you call you can leave your question with an operator and a dietician will call you back within 48 hours with an answer to your question.
CALL BETWEEN 9AM -5PM, **EST** MONDAY-FRIDAY:
1-800-843-8114

FREE HEALTH PUBLICATIONS

The AICR also has a variety of free publications detailed to help you live a healthier lifestyle. A small contribution gets you a very informative newsletter and you can ask for the following booklets by name: *Get Fit, Trim Down-* lose weight sensibly. *Alcohol and Cancer Risk: Make the Choice For Health.* - find out how alcohol affects your cancer risk. *Diet & Cancer* - are you eating enough fiber, something that's been linked to lower cancer risk? *Reducing Your Risk of Colon Cancer* - learn steps you can take that may reduce your risk of one of the most common cancers in the United States. Also ask for *Everything Doesn't Cause Cancer* which will calm many of the concerns you may have about what causes cancer. You can ask for one of these or all.

Write to:
AMERICAN INSTITUTE FOR CANCER RESEARCH
1759 R STREET NW
WASHINGTON, DC 20009
www.aicr.org

HOME HEALTH

This Home Health catalog is the official supplier of Edgar Cayce products for health, beauty and wellness. You'll find over 50 products to help you feel and look your best. There is everything from juices, vitamins, even minerals and salts from the Dead Sea. Write to:
BAAR PRODUCTS
PO BOX 60
DOWNINGTOWN, PA 19335
1-800-269-2502
www.edgarcayce.org

IRON - ESSENTIAL MINERAL

In order to understand the effect that iron and iron deficiency on health development of your baby, this free brochure on iron from Carnation, makers of Good Start Infant Formula, and Follow-Up Formula can answer those questions. Ask for *Iron Brochure*. You'll also learn that although iron is essential for your baby, it is just as essential to a mature adult. Send a SASE to:
CARNATION NUTRITIONAL PRODUCTS
IRON BROCHURE OFFER
PO BOX 65785
SALT LAKE CITY, UT 84165

FAMILY HEALTH RECORD

Every member of the family should keep a medical record. The family's medical record will be useful to you in filling out insurance forms, as well as school and travel records. It can also be vital in helping a physician diagnose a medical problem a family member might have. If you would like they will also send you information on prenatal & natal care, guide to healthy pregnancy and information on how your baby grows. They also have informative brochures for teens about drugs and sexually transmitted disease. Write to:

MARCH OF DIMES
1275 MAMARONECK AVE.
WHITE PLAINS, NY 10605
www.modimes.org

VISUALLY HANDICAPPED

A great series of publications are free to those with Impaired vision. Printed in very large type are instructions for knitting, crocheting, gardening, children's books, etc. Also available are guides for the partially sighted including a dial operator personal directory. There are also 2 free newsletters—*IN FOCUS* for youths and *SEEING CLEARLY* for adults. For a complete listing write:

NATIONAL ASSOCIATION FOR VISUALLY HANDICAPPED
22 WEST 21ST STREET
NEW YORK, NY 10010
(IN CALIF. ONLY—3201 BALBOA ST., SAN FRANCISCO,
CA 94121)
WWW.NAVH.ORG

JOHNSON & JOHNSON HOTLINE

Who can a consumer turn to for answers to their questions concerning hygiene, personal care and baby care? To help you with these questions Johnson & Johnson has set up a toll-free consumer information hotline you can call. Call them with your questions Monday thru Friday between the hours of 8:00am to 6:00pm EST.

THEIR TOLL-FREE HOTLINE IS:
1-800-526-3967
OR CHECK THEIR WEB SITE:
WWW.JNJ.COM

HEARING LOSS

Straight Talk About Hearing Loss, is a fact-filled book about hearing loss and hearing aids. If you're con-

cerned about hearing loss, get the facts about Miracle-Ear. For your free book, call:
1-800-582-2911

HELP FOR THE DEAF

Every year over 200,000 children are born deaf or suffer hearing loss in their first years of life. *Speech and Hearing Checklist* tells parents how to detect possible deafness in their children. Another nice booklet, *Listen! Hear!* is for parents of children who may be deaf or hard of hearing. Both are free from:
ALEXANDER GRAHAM BELL ASSOCIATION FOR THE DEAF
3417 VOLTA PL. N.W.
WASHINGTON, DC 20007
WWW.AGBELL.ORG

HEALTHY BONES

Supplements can help replace calcium that the years take away. Just two of these soft chewy, vanilla-flavored squares give you 1200 mg of calcium daily. For more information on keeping your bones healthy and staying fit, call toll free weekdays between 9:00am and 5:00pm EST:
1-800-STAY-FIT

FREE MEDICAL SUPPLY CATALOG

You can order your medical supplies from your home by phone and save up to 60%. Send for this free catalog from America's leading mail order medical supply catalog. Drop a postcard to:
BRUCE MEDICAL SUPPLY
DEPARTMENT 712
411 WAVERLY OAKS RD.
WALTHAM. MA 02154
1-800-225-8446
WWW.BRUCEMEDICAL.COM
ALSO, BE SURE TO GET A COPY OF THE DISCOUNT
HEALTHCARE CATALOG FREE FROM:
DR. LEONARDS HEALTH CARE PRODUCTS
1-800-785-0880
www.drleonards.com

FAMILY PLANNING ASSISTANCE

For years Planned Parenthood has provided important information dealing with making intelligent family planning decisions. Ask for *Planned Parenthood Guide, Your Contraceptive Choices* and *Sex & Disease - What You Need To Know."* Send a postcard to:

PLANNED PARENTHOOD
810 7TH AVE.
NEW YORK. NY 10019

INFANT CARE HOTLINE

Being a new parent can be quite unsettling. Now there is someone you can call for help. Beech Nut Baby Foods has set up a toll-free hotline you can call. You will receive expert advice on infant care from a pediatrician, child psychologist, dentist or nutritionist. If you are about to have a child or have recently had one be sure to ask for the *"new parent packet"* and also for information about their label-saving program where you can exchange product UPC labels for discount coupons. Call between the hours of 9am and 8pm E.S.T. weekdays:
1-800-523-6633

MEDICARE HOTLINE

If you have questions or problems regarding Medicare, now there's a toll-free number you can call for help. When you call you can get additional information regarding a Medicare claim you may have, general information about Medicare and the services it provides. They can also help you with information regarding insurance supplements to Medicare, mammograms and lots more. Call:
1-800-638-6833
www.medicare.com

SEXUALLY TRANSMITTED DISEASES HOTLINE

If you suspect you may have contracted a sexually transmitted disease, there's a toll free hotline you can call for help and for information. Their specialists will answer your questions concerning STDs and tell you the symptoms that are the warning signs of disease and how to get help. You'll be referred to free or low-cost public health clinics or

doctors in your area. They will also send you free brochures concerning STDs. Call Monday thru Friday between 8AM and 8PM. at:
1-800-227-8922
www.cdc.gov

HIV & AIDS HOTLINE

If you have or suspect you may have contracted HIV, there's a toll-free number you can call in confidence for help and for information concerning HIV and AIDS. Call:
1-800-342-2437

HEART DIET

If you would like a copy of the American Heart Association recommendations including lists of good and bad foods, and practical suggestions for cutting out the bad stuff. Ask for *Exercise Your Heart; An Eating Plan For Healthy Americans; Cholesterol & Your Heart* and *Recipes For Low-Fat, Low Cholesterol Meals.* Send a SASE to:
AMERICAN HEART ASSOCIATION, NATIONAL CENTER
7272 GREENVILLE AVE
DALLAS, TX 75231
1-800-242-8721
www.americanheart.org

HELP FOR ALCOHOLICS & THEIR FAMILIES

Alcoholism is a disease and can be cured. AA wants to help anyone who has (or suspects they have) a drinking problem. Find out what AA is and how it can help - ask for their *information package.* All literature comes in an unmarked envelope. Write to:
A A
BOX 459
GRAND CENTRAL STATION
NEW YORK, NY 10163

And if you're in a disfunctional relationship with an alcholic or know a teen whose parent is an alcoholic, be sure to contact:
AL-ANON FAMILY GROUP HEADQUARTERS

1600 Corporate Landing Parkway
Virginia Beach, VA 23454-5617
Web site: www.al-anon-alateen.org

SKIN PROTECTION

Prevention is always far better than a cure. For a free booklet *Skin Cancer: If You Can Spot It You Can Stop It,* send a long SASE to:
The Skin Cancer Foundation
245 Fifth Ave. Suite 1403
New York, NY 10016
1-800-SKIN-490
www.skincancer.org

TREATING STROKES

For up-to-date information on strokes and effective treatment and therapy for those who fall victim to a stroke, ask for your free copy of *Guide To Strokes,* write:
Stroke
NINCDS-W
9000 Rockville Pike, Bldg 31, Rm 8A16
Bethesda, MD 20892

GUIDES TO HEALTHY LIVING

America's pharmaceutical companies would like you to have their *Guides To Healthy Living.* The subjects covered include breast cancer, heart attacks, strokes, menopause, and prostate cancer. For information on any or all of these topics call this information hotline toll-free:
1-800-862-5110

GET FIT !

As part of a program initiated by the President's Council on Physical Fitness and Sports, The Hershey Company has a number of helpful and informative resources that are free for the asking. They are geared to young people ages 6-17. There's even a motivational message from Arnold Schwarzenegger. Learn how to get in shape to meet the presidents challenge. A few of the free items include:
Hershey's Field of Fun - helpful tips for running a field day at school, camp or any

other group program.
Official Rule Book of Hershey's Track & Field
New Softball Rules
National Track & Field Youth Program - information about this great program including rules and regulations.
The Story Behind The Chocolate Bar - The Story of Milton S. Hershey.
Send a long SASE to:
HERSHEY'S YOUTH PROGRAM
HERSHEYS CHOCOLATE
19 EAST CHOCOLATE AVE.
PO BOX 814
HERSHEY, PA 17033

FREE CONTACT LENSES

If you wear contact lenses or are thinking of getting them, Johnson & Johnson would like you to try their Acuvue contacts. They have made arrangements with local optometrist throughout the country to supply you with a your first pair. Just ask an optometrist in your area who carries Acuvue contacts for a free pair.

HEALTH HOTLINES

To help answer various health questions you may have there are a number of toll-free hotlines you can call:
CALCIUM INFORMATION CENTER:
1-800-321-2681
MILK CONSUMER HOTLINE:
1-800-WHY-MILK
NATIONAL CENTER FOR NUTRITION & DIURETICS
1-800-366-1655
NATIONAL OSTEOPEROSIS FOUNDATION
1-800-223-9994
FOOD ALLERGY NETWORK
1-800-929-4040
CONSUMER NUTRITION HOTLINE
1-800-366-1655

THE BLOCH NATIONAL CANCER HOTLINE
THEY WILL PUT YOU IN TOUCH WITH SOMEONE WHO HAS HAD THE SAME TYPE OF CANCER AND WILL HELP YOU DEAL WITH THE INITIAL FEAR. CALL: **1-800-433-0464**

NATIONAL CANCER INSTITUTE

To help you keep informed about the most up-to-date information about cancer, the National Cancer Institute has a toll-free number you can call. When you call you can ask for free publications, or ask for help locating FDA-approved mammography facilities or talk with cancer specialists.

1-800-422-6237

CANCER CARE

Cancer Care provides a wide range of programs for cancer patients and their families. They will also provide pamphlets and *A Helping Hand: The Resource Guide for People with Cancer.* Call:

1-800-813-HOPE

AMERICAN CANCER SOCIETY

They offer referrals to cancer centers across the country, plus free informative booklets on cancer risk reduction and early detection and treatment. Call them toll-free at:

1-800-ACS-2345

NATIONAL ALLIANCE OF BREAST CANCER ORGANIZATIONS

This is a helpful organization if you need referrals to physicians, support groups, speakers and minority health advocates. They also help groups plan breast cancer awareness events. Call:

1-888-80-NABCO

Web site: www.nabco.org

BREAST CANCER

Women need to be fully aware of the signs of breast cancer. The Susan G. Komen Breast Cancer Foundation can help anyone who needs referrals to certified mammography centers, clinical trials and other programs about breast cancer. They will even supply you with free shower cards on breast self-exam to hand out at a baby or wedding shower. What a way to show you care about every one of your guests. They can even supply you with large print

pamphlets and cards *Taking Charge: Breast Health for Older Women*. If you have any questions or want specific information, call them at:
1-800-IMAWARE

BEATING THE SILENT KILLER

Ovarian cancer is a silent killer and very often a woman doesn't have a warning sign that she has symptoms until it's too late. That's why it is important to have a check up and learn to identify those warning signs. Send for your free copy of *It Whispers... So Listen, What Every Woman Should Know About Ovarian Cancer*, send a self addressed stamped envelope to:

**NATIONAL OVARIAN CANCER COALITION
2335 EAST ATLANTIC BLVD., SUITE 401
POMPANO BEACH, FL 33062**

STOPPING SKIN CANCER BEFORE IT STARTS

Skin cancer can lead to disfigurement or even death once it has spread to other parts of the body. But if treated early, it is almost always curable. Self examination of your skin every three months is the best way to detect any abnormalities. To help you look for unusual marks, growths or changes on your skin, the Skin Cancer Foundation will send you a free brochure that includes a body map and warning signs of all major skin cancers. You'll even receive a free sample of Oil of Olay moisture cream with UV protectant. Send a long self addressed stamped envelope to:

**THE SKIN CANCER FOUNDATION
245 FIFTH AVE. SUITE 1403
NEW YORK, NY 10016
www.skincancer.org**

PROTECING YOUR SKIN

Remember that being out in the sun is a healthy thing to do, as long as you protect your skin from the damaging rays of the sun. The American Academy of Dermatology has some valuable tips for you next to you venture out. Ask for *Protect Your Skin From the Sun*. Call toll-free:
1-888-462-3376 OR WRITE:

AMERICAN ACADEMY OF DERMATOLOGY
930 N. MEACHAM RD.,
SCHAUMBURG, IL, 60173
Web site: www.aad.org

AMERICAN SOCIETY OF CLINICAL ONCOLOGY

The American Society of Clinical Oncology has extensive information about cancer on its web site that covers everything from local resources to clinical trials. For more information, log onto:
www.asco.org

DRUG INTERACTIONS

Some times when someone is taking more than one prescription drug, the particular combination of drugs may produce an adverse reaction. If you suspect a you may have problem coming from drug interaction, let your doctor know. You can report adverse interactions to the Food and Drug Administrations MedWatch by calling:
1-888-463-6332
For a reporting forum or to download information online go to:
www.fda.gov/medwatch

CLEARING UP CATARACTS

A cataract is a clouding of the eye's natural lens. In cataract surgery the lens is removed and replaced with an implant to restore vision. For the most part, implants are designed to give good vision at one distance, usually far, so you would need glasses for reading. Now, Array Multifocal lens implant is designed to provide good distance and near vision. If you want to learn more about this procedure call:
1-888-459-7847
www.arraylens.com

PESTICIDES AND FOOD SAFETY

Did you ever wonder what makes that delicious red apple so shiny and slick? Well if it looks as if it's been sealed with a shiny coat of wax, maybe it has been. Fruits and vegetables in some instances (unless they are organically grown) go through processes where they are coated to protect them against insects and other pests until they are harvested and shipped to market. If you want to learn more about pesticides and food safety write and ask for this very informative guide: *A Consumer's Guide to Pesticides and Food Safety.* Send a SASE to:

INTERNATIONAL FOOD INFORMATION COUNCIL FOUNDATION
100 CONNECTICUT AVE., NW, SUITE 430
WASHINGTON, DC 20036

HIGH BLOOD PRESSURE

Learn about high blood pressure and its effects on the body. The National Kidney Foundation has a free book just for the asking. Ask for *High Blood Pressure and Your Kidneys.* Write to:

NATIONAL KIDNEY FOUNDATION
30 E. 33RD ST.
NEW YORK, NY 10016

SNACK TIME

Do you like to snack but are worried about what those sweets do to your teeth? If so you'll want to send for this free copy of *Snack Smart for Healthy Teeth*. Learn more about tasty snacks that won't harm your teeth. Ask for *Snack Smart for Healthy Teeth*. Write to:

NATIONAL INSTITUTE OF DENTAL AND CRANIOFACIAL RESEARCH
31 CENTER DR. MSC 2290
BETHESDA, MD 20892-2290

FREE FOR ALLERGY SUFFERERS

Over 40 millions people suffer from annoying seasonal nasal allergies with symptoms that include sneezing, running nose and congestion. If that describes you, you might want to ask your doctor about Nasonex spray. If he prescribes it, you can get a free one month trial offer directly from the manufacturer. This is a limited time offer so write today to:

NASONEX TRIAL OFFER
SCHERING LABORATORIES
KENILWORTH, NJ 07033

LIFE WITHOUT ALLERGIES

If you are bothered by allergies you know how that fact can dominate your life. The American College

of Allergy, Asthma and Immunology has a free brochure for you called, *You Can Have A Life Without Allergies.* To get your copy simply call:
1-800-842-7777
Or visit their web site at:
http://allergy.mcg.edu

ALLERGY RELIEF

Do you suffer from seasonal or year round nasal allergies? Then you'll want to learn more about nasal allergies and how you can get relief. The makers of Flonase want you to know the facts by sending your their brochure, *Feel-Better Facts About Nasal Allergies.* Along with this important information you will receive a $5.00-off coupon your first prescription. They will also send you a free allergy newsletter, *Allergy Talk,* to keep you more informed. If you suffer from nasal allergies don't wait, call:
1-800-FLONASE
Or visit their website at: www.glaxowellcome.com

SURGERY QUESTIONS

If you are considering having any type of non-emergency surgery, be sure to get your free copy of *Questions to Ask Your Doctor Before Surgery.* It will help you be informed about the options and risks involved. Call toll-free:
1-800-358-9295

HOW GOOD IS YOUR DOCTOR?

Want to check your doctor's track record? It's important to find out if the specialist or doctor you search out is board-certified in his specialty. Here are several web sites that will help you with this search. On the Internet, to find if the doctor is actually certified in his specialty, search:
www.certified-doctor.com
Also to get biographies and malpractice information, check with DocFinder at:
www.docboard.org

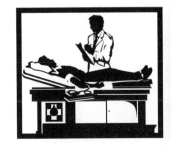

There is also a huge resource called 16,638 *Questionable Doctors* put out by the Public Citizens Health Research Group. It lists doctors who have lost their licenses, or who have been fined or suspended. Check this out on the Web at:
www.citizen.org

HEALTH ANSWERS ONLINE

Dr. Koop, the former Surgeon General, has an outstanding web site you will want to visit for the latest news on all health-related subjects. At this site you will find a wealth of information on wellness, nutrition, fitness and prevention as well as current information on over 50 health topics ranging from Alzheimer's disease to cancer, diabetes, heart disease and migraine. You can also sign up for their free Newsletter which they will e-mail directly to you. You will also find links to prescription drug sites where you can purchase medicine and vitamins quickly, easily and at terrific savings. Visit their web site at:
www.drkoop.com

PROGRESSIVE EYE CARE

If you wear bifocals or need several pairs of glasses to see correctly at different distances, you may want to consider Varilux lenses. Known as progressive lenses, Varilux take bifocals to a new level giving you various degrees of correction in one set of lenses. For free information call them toll-free at:
1-800-VARILUX

LYME'S TOLL-FREE HEALTH LINE

For information on Lyme disease, call the National Lyme Disease Foundation at:
1-800-886-LYME

NATIONAL INSTITUTES OF NEUROLOGICAL DISORDERS AND STROKE

For information on treatment and research on strokes and neurological disorders, check out this web site and then click on "health information"
www.ninds.nih.gov

AMERICAN PARKINSON DISEASE

For information on this disease, local referrals, support groups, research funding, call:
1-800-223-2732
or visit their web site:
www.apdaparkinson.com

Free For Kids

FREE CIRCUS TICKETS

If your child was born in the U.S. in the last year, he or she is entitled to a free ticket to a Ringling Brothers & Barnum & Bailey Circus redeemable any time in his/her lifetime. To get their free ticket, parents only need visit their web site and provide their newborn's name, address, and date of birth:

FELD ENTERTAINMENT

Register online at: www.ringling.com and click on 'Special Offers'

COMIC BOOK

The American Cancer Society would love to send you a free SpiderMan comic book. SpiderMan and his webbed buddies battle the evil villain Smokescreen in a vivid, and exciting antismoking comic. To get this free comic book ask for the *Spiderman Comic Book*. Call The American Cancer Society at:

1-800-227-2345

FREE COLORING BOOK

If you've ever wanted to know more about your lungs, and have fun while doing it this free offer is for you. You have your choice of three books, an activity book, a coloring book, or a crossword puzzle book. Specify the books you want or ask for the *"facts about smoking"* package: *Smoking...Lungs At Work* #0840; *Second-Hand Smoke; Let's Solve The Smokeword* puzzle-book, #0043. Send it on a postcard to:

AMERICAN LUNG ASSOCIATION

BOX 596

NEW YORK, NY 10116

MONEY MANAGEMENT FOR TEENAGERS

Consumer Federation of America has a helpful guide that will help you to teach your teenager responsible money management. This is a must for every parent. Send a SASE to:

CONSUMER FEDERATION OF AMERICA
1424 16TH ST. NW, SUITE 604
WASHINGTON, DC 20036

"SCIENCE WEEKLY"

An introduction to the wonderful world of science. Science Weekly, will send you a free sample copy of their newsletter- written specifically for kids. It's an easy read and touches on important topics involving science and is written for kids (grades K - 8th) in order to bring them a better understanding of the sciences, languages and even mathematics. Write and specify which grade level you want when you write to:

SCIENCE WEEKLY
SUBSCRIPTION DEPT.
PO BOX 70154
WASHINGTON, DC 20088

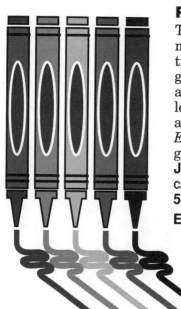

FREE COLORING BOOKS

The makers of Triaminic cough and cold medicines is giving away two free educational coloring books. These two books are great and help kids to learn and understand about illnesses such as Alzheimer's, epilepsy and diabetes. They offer descriptions and excellent explanations. Ask for: *Kid's Educational Coloring Books* (specify English or Spanish). Write to:

JEFF'S COMPANION ANIMAL SHELTER
c/o SANDOZ PHARMACEUTICALS
59 ROUTE 10

E. HANOVER, NJ 07936

YO YO TRICKS

This easy to understand, illustrated pamphlet teaches you the "ancient -art" of 'Yo Yo Trickery." Learn some of the same tricks that made the Yo Yo famous, like Walking the

Dog, the Spinner, The Creeper, Loop the Loop and lots more. You'll be learning the fun tournament tricks in no time. Ask for *"Yo Yo Trick Pamphlet."* Send a SASE to:
DUNCAN TOYS CO.
PO BOX 5
MIDDLEFIELD, OH 44062

OWLIE SKYWARN
What can you do to make yourself safe from lightning, tornadoes and hurricanes? Owlie Skywarn has two freebies you will want to have:
1. *"Hurricanes & Tornados* - tells about the causes and devastating effects of storms, hurricanes and tornados.
2. "Owlie Skywarn Weather Book" - learn exactly what weather is and what causes the changes in seasons.
For your free copies write:
NATIONAL LOGISTICS SUPPORT CENTER
1510 EAST BANNISTER RD. BLDG. #1
KANSAS CITY, MO 64131

ENERGY INFORMATION
Everyone must do their share to save energy. The Conservation & Renewable Energy Inquiry & Referral Service (CAREIRS) has a nice information package any youngster would love to have: Learn what you can do to conserve energy. Excellent! And it's yours free from:
CAREIRS
PO BOX 3048
MERRIFIELD, VA 22116.

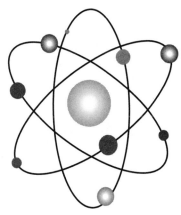

FUN-FILLED CATALOG
If you'd like a copy of what is probably the most unusual and funfilled catalog in the world, send for the *Things You Never Knew Existed* catalog. It is filled with 1600 novelties, gadgets and fun-makers of every type. Send a postcard to:
JOHNSON SMITH CO.,
4514 19TH COURT E.
BRADENTON, FL 34203
1-800-843-0762
www.johnsonsmith.com

DON'T GET HOOKED

The Office on Smoking and Health has a variety of colorful posters and interesting material explaining the real dangers of smoking. Ask for their free catalog of informative materials on smoking and your health. After you receive the catalog you can request the specific free materials you want. Send a postcard to:

OFFICE ON SMOKING AND HEALTH
PARK BLDG., 1-58
ROCKVILLE, MD 20857

TAKE A BITE OUT OF CRIME

The crime detective dog, McGruff will show you what you can do to fight crime. McGruff and his nephew, Scruff will send you a fun comic/activity book that will show your children how to make themselves and their friends safer. They also have a *Parent's Streetwise Kids Guide.* Ask for *Scruff McGruff Take a Bite Out of Crime.*
Write to:

NATIONAL CRIME PREVENTION COUNCIL
1700 K STREET N.W. 2ND FLOOR
WASHINGTON, D.C. 20006-3817

Also, for a free action kit packed with ideas and real life experiences of what neighbors working together can do to prevent crime and make you and your family safer, call:

1-800-WE-PREVENT   (that's **1-800-937-7383**

SHARK TOOTH FOSSIL

Here is your chance to learn some amazing facts about sharks. You'll receive one genuine shark tooth fossil and a fact sheet about sharks and their teeth. To get yours, write 'shark tooth' on a piece of paper and send a long self-addressed stamped envelope with $1.00 (no checks please), to:

EDINBORO CREATIONS
DEPT. T-1
1210 BRIERLY LANE
MUNHALL, PA 15120

ARROWHEAD

How did people hunt and protect themselves thousands of years ago? Send for this genuine hand-chipped arrowhead and find out! To send for your arrowhead print the word *arrowhead* on a piece of paper and send a long self-addressed stamped envelope with $1.00 (no checks please), to:

EDINBORO CREATIONS
DEPT. A-1
1210 BRIERLY LANE
MUNHALL, PA 15120

INSTANT MILLIONAIRE

You too can be a millionaire! Show off your million dollar bill. It's not real money-but you'll have a ball showing it off.. Print your request for a million dollar bill on a slip of paper, put it in a large self-addressed stamped envelope with $1.00 (no checks please) and send it to:

THE RICH GORILLA   DEPT 1
1210 COMMONWEALTH AVE.
MUNHALL, PA 15120

BOOKMARK

This awesome bookmark assigns an Egyptian hieroglyphic to each letter of the alphabet. Now you can code your own messages! To send for your Egyptian Bookmark send a long self-addressed stamped envelope along with $1.00 (no checks please) to:

EDINBORO CREATIONS
DEPT. EGB-1
1210 BRIERLY LANE
MUNGALL, PA 15120

COOL NOTE PADS

These super cool note pads are the neatest way to write notes, messages or even secret messages. To receive a selection of assorted note pads write the word note pad on a sheet of paper and send it with a long self-addressed stamped envelope. Don't forget to include 50 cents (no checks please). Send your request to:

JACOB T
DEPT 1
1210 COMMONWEALTH AVE.
MUNHALL, PA 15120

LAPIS LAZULI

Lapis Lazuli was the favorite gemstone of the Egyptian pharaohs. Now you can own an oval stone weighing about two-and-a-half carats, perfect for jewelry making or gem collecting.. To get yours, write the word 'lapis lazuli' on a sheet of paper and send it with a long self-addressed stamped envelope and $1.00 (no checks please) to:

EDINBORO CREATIONS
DEPT 1
1210 BRIERLY LANE
MUNGHALL, PA 15120

GEMSTONE COLLECTION

If you ever wanted to start a gemstone collection here's your chance. You will receive three genuine oval stones, including rose quartz, snowflake obsidian, and tiger-eye. Each stone weighs about two carats. To receive yours just write the word gemstone collection on a piece of paper and send it with a long self-addressed stamped envelope with $1.00 (no checks please) to:

EDINBORO CREATIONS
DEPT. 1
1210 BRIERLY LANE
MUNHALL, PA 15120

SCRATCH-AND-SNIFF PAINT

Did you ever want to paint ? Now you can create your own masterpiece, and express yourself with paint you can see and smell. You'll receive one cool paintbrush and instructions to make scratch -and - sniff watercolors. To get your kit simply write the words scratch-and-sniff paint instructions on a sheet of paper, include a long self-addressed stamped envelope and 25 cents (no checks please) to:

THE PAINTING GORILLA
DEPT. 1
1210 COMMONWEALTH AVE.
MUNHALL, PA 15120

Religion

CATHOLIC INFORMATION

The Knights of Columbus has dozens of booklets available on all aspects of the Catholic religion. The only cost is a nominal postage charge (generally 35¢ per booklet). They also have a 10 part home-study Catholic correspondence course that is free for the asking. The course is for both Catholics and non-Catholics who would like to learn more about Catholicism. It is sent in an unmarked envelope. For a complete *listing of publications* or to get your free correspondence course write to:

CATHOLIC INFORMATION SERVICE
KNIGHTS OF COLUMBUS
BOX 1971
NEW HAVEN, CT 06521

DAILY INSPIRATION

Our Daily Bread" provides inspirational readings from the scriptures for each day of the month. You'll get a new book each month. Ask them to add your name to their mailing list for this devotional guide plus discovery series booklets as well as a campus journal for young people. All free from:

RADIO BIBLE CLASS
P.O. BOX 2222
GRAND RAPIDS, MI 49555

NEWS NOTES

These *News Notes* are published by the Christophers 10 times a year and are free for the asking. The Christophers exist for one purpose: to spread the message that one person can make a difference in this world. Write and ask for information on titles available in any of these categories, News Note, books, videocassettes, they even have Spanish language issues. Drop a postcard to :

THE CHRISTOPHERS
12 EAST 48TH ST.
NEW YORK, NY 10017

INSPIRATION AND PRAYER

The Lutheran Laymen's League has several religious publications you might like to have. A few of the titles currently available are: *Escape From Loneliness; I Am An Alcoholic; Stress - Problem or Opportunity?* and *The Truth About Angels.* All free from:
INTERNATIONAL LUTHERAN LAYMEN'S LEAGUE
2185 HAMPTON AVE.
ST. LOUIS, MO 63139

POWER FOR LIVING

The folks at the Arthur S. DeMoss Foundation would like to know that God gives us the power for living on a daily basis. They have put together an inspiring collection of messages from the bible into a book called *Power For Living.* No contributions will be solicited or accepted and no one will call you. To get your copy, call:
1-800-341-5000

FREE LIFE OF CHRIST VIDEO

The Church of Latter Day Saints have a beautiful video they would like to send you depicting the life of Jesus Christ, His life and His message. To get your copy of this video simply call:
1-800-519-1551

FREE FROM THE WORLDWIDE CHURCH OF GOD

The Worldwide Church of God has an excellent series of booklets available without charge (nor will they make any solicitations of any kind). Titles change frequently so drop a card for a current list of books available. Write to:
WORLDWIDE CHURCH OF GOD
PASADENA, CA 91123
OR CALL TOLL-FREE: **1-800-423-4444**

BEAUTIFUL INSPIRATION

Often in our daily lives events become too much to handle. The Salesian Missions have a beautiful series of booklets that are a pleasure to read and provide inspiration to help make our lives more

fulfilling. Excellent! Drop a card for the *free inspirational booklets* from:
SALESIAN MISSIONS
2 LEFEVRES LANE
NEW ROCHELLE, NY 10801

FAMILY ANSWERS

If you have teenagers you already know how difficult it is to talk to them without getting into an argument. Now with the free *Family Answers* video from the Mormons you will find concrete tips on improving communication between parents and teens. For your free copy of this helpful video, call:
1-800-519-1551

GOSPEL OF JOHN COURSE

If you would like to learn more about the life of Christ, you can receive a free Gospel of John in English or Spanish (please specify) and a *Gospel of John Correspondence Course*. Drop a postcard to:
THE POCKET TESTAMENT LEAGUE
PO BOX 800
LITITZ, PA 17543

FREE KING JAMES BIBLE

If you would like a 764 page copy of the King James version of the Bible, it's yours free from The Church of Jesus Christ of Latter Day Saints...The Mormons. For your free copy (which will be sent by mail), call:
1-800-535-1118

BIBLE READING GUIDES

For a new understanding of the Bible, you may want to receive simplified *Bible Reading Guides* yours free from the Real Truth Ministries. To enroll in this bible course, call toll free:
1-800-863-5789

Learning Can Be Fun

U.S. MONETARY SYSTEM

How much do you really know about how the U.S. economy works? Do you know what the Federal Reserve System is or how it helps our monetary system work? For answers to these and other questions, get a copy of *Too Much, Too Little*. Put out by the Federal Reserve and geared to high school grade levels, it explains in comic book format just how the Federal Reserve helps keep out economy strong. Free from:

FEDERAL RESERVE BANK OF NY—PUBLICATIONS DEPT.
FEDERAL RESERVE PO STATION
NEW YORK, NY 10045-0001

SKY GAZERS

If you enjoy studying the heavens, you will want to get a copy of Essential Magazines of Astronomy with a catalog of some of the finest astronomy books that will delight all star gazers. Write to:

SKY PUBLISHING CORP.
49 BAY STREET RD.
CAMBRIDGE, MA 02138
1-800-253-0245
www.skyandtelescope.com

LOOK TO THE HEAVENS

Man has always been fascinated by the sky at night. With the recent discovery of planets circling around distant stars, one can't help but wonder whether life exists elsewhere in the universe. To find out more about our distant neighbors, send for the *skywatching series of booklets* dealing with our solar system and beyond. Send to:

PUBLIC AFFAIRS OFFICE
HARVARD SMITHSONIAN CENTER FOR ASTROPHYSICS
60 GARDEN ST.
CAMBRIDGE, MA 02138
www.harvard.edu

QUARTER HORSES

Whether you are presently an owner of horses or perhaps thinking of buying one - check out American Quarter Horses, the world's most popular breed of horse. Here's an interesting booklet you will want to have: *For An American Quarter Horse.* For a copy of this fascinating booklet (and a colorful bumper sticker too), drop a card to:

AMERICAN QUARTER HORSE ASSN.
PO Box 200
AMARILLO, TX 79168
WWW.AQHA.COM

TENNESSEE WALKING HORSE

Here's one every equestrian will want to have. Send a card for the *Tennessee Walking Horse* plus a colorful postcard showing the three horses chosen by the breeder's association as the world's greatest pleasure and show horse. Write to:

TENNESSEE WALKING HORSE
Box 286
LEWISBURG, TN 37091-0286
1-800-359-1574
www.twhbea.com

PARENT'S GUIDE TO CYBERSPACE

The Internet has opened us all to a new world. At the touch of a keyboard you can watch a volcano come to life, read a story to your child, view an original copy of Lincoln's Gettysburg address or instantly send a letter to a friend across the country or on the other side of the world. For a free copy of the *Librarian's Guide to Cyberspace for Parents & Kids,"* request it from:

AMERICAN LIBRARY ASSOCIATION INFORMATION OFFICE
50 EAST HURON ST DEPT P
CHICAGO, IL 60611

And be sure to visit their terrific web site:

www.ala.org/parentspage/greatsites

where you'll find 700+ "amazing, spectacular, mysterious, colorful web sites for kids and the adults who care about them."

KEEP IN MIND: If you don't have a computer or Internet access at home, most libraries have computers you can use and educational programs for children and adults to teach you how to use them.

AUSTRALIA

AUSTRALIA TODAY

What is life like 'down-under'? *Australia Now* will give you a look—in full color-at what's happening in Australia today. You'll also receive vacation planning, travel tips and information on locations, tours and accommodations. Drop a postcard to:

AUSTRALIAN CONSULATE GENERAL
630 FIFTH AVE. SUITE 420
NEW YORK NY 10111

SELF IMPROVEMENT

Would you like to take charge of your life — control your smoking, lose weight, attract more love or make more money? Maybe you should look through the *Love Tapes catalog*. Based on sound psychological principles, these tapes will help you develop your full potential. Send a card to:

EFFECTIVE LEARNING SYSTEMS
5221 EDINA IND BLVD.
EDINA, MN 55434

HOME FIRE DETECTION

Learn how to protect your family and your home with smoke detectors—a must for all homes. Send a card to:

"HOME FIRE DETECTION,"
NATIONAL FIRE PROTECTION ASSOCIATION
BATTERYMARCH PARK
QUINCY, MA 02269

A SHARE OF AMERICA

Getting Help When You Invest and *Understanding Stocks and Bonds* and two fascinating guides that tells all about how the stock market works and the important role it plays in our nation's economy. The New York Stock Exchange also has an excellent series of educational aids, huge wall posters, ticker tape, teacher guides and more. Incidentally teachers can get a package tailored to the grade level they're teaching. Quantities of books will be supplied for each student. Write to:

N.Y. STOCK EXCHANGE
EDUCATIONAL SERVICES
11 WALL ST.
NEW YORK, NY 10005
www.nyse.com

THE WRIGHT BROTHERS

With men on the moon and rockets to Jupiter it's hard to believe that manned flight began just 100 years ago with an historic 120 foot journey that lasted all of 12 seconds. All the fascinating details are found in this historical recap called, *Wright Brothers*. Send a postcard to:

WRIGHT BROTHERS NATIONAL MEMORIAL
ROUTE 1, BOX 676
MANTEO, NC 27954

TRUTH ABOUT NUCLEAR ENERGY

Is nuclear energy the answer to our energy needs or are the risks of nuclear disaster just too great? To help you answer this question, here is an excellent package of books that is free for the asking. Topics covered include nuclear power plants, the structure of the atom, magnetic fusion, the story of nuclear energy and a whole lot more. They will also include information about wind energy and conservation. Ask for the *Nuclear Energy information package*. It's very informative and it's free from:

U.S. DEPARTMENT OF ENERGY
PO BOX 62
OAK RIDGE, TN 37830

STORY OF COTTON

Here's a huge wall poster with colorful illustrations showing the development of cotton from seed to clothing. Also included will be an interesting book on cotton. The kids will love this. *The Story of Cotton* poster is yours free from:

NATIONAL COTTON COUNCIL
PO BOX 12285
MEMPHIS, TN 38112

FACTS ABOUT OIL

This nicely illustrated guide to petroleum tells all about the history of oil exploration and shows how the search for oil is conducted. Ask for the *"energy information series"* and you'll receive a great package of excellent booklets dealing with many forms of energy including wind, nuclear, geothermal, coal, oil and more. Send a card to:
AMERICAN PETROLEUM INSTITUTE
PUBLICATIONS SECTION
1220 L ST. N.W.
WASHINGTON, DC 20005
www.api.org

THE REAL DEAL

Everyone spends money, but not everyone knows how to do it right. Spending money wisely takes skill, time and experience. To help you learn how to shop smart, the FTC and the National Association of Attorneys General have put together a fun activity booklet called *The Real Deal.* To get your free copy, write to:
YOUR STATE ATTORNEY GENERAL
OFFICE OF CONSUMER PROTECTION
YOUR STATE CAPITAL
OR TO: THE FEDERAL TRADE COMMISSION
600 PENNSYLVANIA AVE., NW, ROOM 130
WASHINGTON, DC 20580
1-877-FTC-HELP
WWW.FTC.GOV

BE A BETTER WRITER

The National Council of Teachers of English have compiled some handy tips to help make your children better writers. If they start with good writing skills as early as possible, they will have no problem with the written word later on. Ask for *How to Help Your Child Become A Better Writer.* Specify English or Spanish edition. Send a SASE to:
NATIONAL COUNCIL OF TEACHERS OF ENGLISH
DEPT. C, 1111 KENYON RD.
URBANA, IL 61801

ALUMINUM CARS?

Today, through greater use of aluminum parts our cars are getting far better miles per gallon. This is just one of the many uses of aluminum. If you would like a better understanding of the history of aluminum, the ways it is made and how it's used, ask for the free *Story of Aluminum* and *Alcoa* from:

ALCOA
150 ALCOA BUILDING.
PITTSBURGH, PA 15219
www.alcoa.com

CLEAN ENVIRONMENT

Bethlehem Steel would like you to know what they are doing to clean up the air and water. For example, at one plant they have spent over 100 million dollars for air and water quality controls. For a free copy of *"Steelmaking & The Environment,"* send a card to:

BETHLEHEM STEEL CORP.
PUBLIC AFFAIRS DEPT., ROOM 476MT
BETHLEHEM, PA 18016

CHAMBER OF COMMERCE

What Is the Chamber of Commerce? Who runs it? What does it do? For a concise booklet answering your questions, write to:

CHAMBER OF COMMERCE OF THE U.S.
1615 H ST. N.W.
WASHINGTON, DC 20062

PITCH THIS ONE!

If you have ever thought about taking up horse shoe pitching, now's the time. (Did you know that former President George Bush used to pitch horseshoes?) To find out more about this fun sport and to learn all the rules and tips for throwing the perfect horseshoe pitch. Send for your free copy of the *Official Rules For Horseshoe Pitching.* Send a SASE to:

NHPA, RR2
BOX 178
LAMONTE, MD 65337

MAZES

If you like puzzles and mazes, you will love this freebie. You will receive a complimentary 11" x 17" maze valued at $2.95. Send $1.00 for postage and handling and ask for it from:

PDK ENTERPRISES
PO BOX 1776
BOYES HOT SPRINGS, CA 95416

FREE SAMPLE SCIENCE PROJECT PLAN

If you enjoy doing science experiments, this one's for you. You'll receive 9 sample science project Instruction Plans including: Volcano model, microwave effects on seeds, testing biodegradables, synthetic cola plus five more. They list materials needed and gives instruction about how to do the project. Includes a full listing of 265 others available at nominal cost. Great for science students and teachers. Send a name & address label and $2.00 postage and handling to:

SCIENCESOUTH
PO BOX 50182
KNOXVILLE, TN 37950

LEARNING TO BE MORE ROMANTIC

Since the beginning of time, women have accused men of not being romantic. Finally there's help and it's called *The RoMANtic*. Each 12 page newsletter gives dozens of practical, creative and inspiring ideas and stories on dating, gift-giving, anniversary celebrating and more. To learn how to rekindle the romantic spark and have more fun in your relationships, send 3 first class stamps to:

THE ROMANTIC SAMPLE ISSUE OFFER
714 COLLINGTON DR.
CARY, NC 27511

OR CHECK OUT SAMPLE ISSUES AT THEIR WEB site:
www.theromantic.com

RAISING CHILDREN DRUG FREE

One of the most important concerns every parent has is how to raise their children free of drugs and the abusive use of alcohol. Developing strong loving relationships with our children is essential as is teaching proper standards of right and wrong and setting and enforcing rules. Equally important is teaching children the facts about alcohol and drugs. If you are a parent, you will absolutely want to get a free copy of *Growing Up Drug Free....A Parent's Guide To Prevention.* In this excellent guide you will find very specific activities and lessons, full color photos and descriptions of drugs and drug paraphernalia. It comes to you from the Department of Education. Call them toll-free at: **1-800-624-0100**

ALL ABOUT MINING
America has been blessed with enormous amounts of natural resources that enrich our lives all thanks to the people in our mining industry. Teachers will love, *What Mining Means to Americans* which is a fascinating look at this important industry. Write to:
NATIONAL MINING ASSOCIATION
1130 17TH ST. N.W.
WASHINGTON, DC 20036-4677

LEARN ABOUT COAL
If you're a teacher or a student interested in finding out more about coal and how it is found, extracted, transported and used, be sure to get the informative booklets and poster available free from the American Coal Foundation. When you write, be sure to indicate your organization or school, grade level, and phone number so they can provide appropriate materials for you. A few of the items available include:
Coal Poster - A large colorful poster with important coal information
Coal: Ancient Gift Serving Modern Man
Let's Learn About Coal - includes puzzles and word games explain how coal is formed.
What Everyone Should Know About Coal - Describes the different types of coal, how it is used and how it effects the envirnment.
Coal Science Fair Ideas - to help spark interest in coal plus tips to help you get started with a project. Write to:
AMERICAN COAL FOUNDATION
1130 17TH ST NW, SUITE 220
WASHINGTON, DC 20036-4604
Or visit their web site: www.acf-coal.org

Money for College & Beyond

FREE COLLEGE AID

There are literally billions of millions of dollars in financial aid available to help students pay for their college education. This money is available from thousands of public and private sources. Much of this money is available as outright grants that never has to be repaid. Still more money for college is available through low-cost loans and work-study programs. The first place to check is with the financial aid office of the college of your choice. Counselors will help you locate all the sources of money including scholarships, grant-in-aid, work study programs and low interest government-backed student loans. Other sources of assistance are listed below.

GETTING MONEY FOR COLLEGE

Sallie Mae is the leading source of money for college loans. They can help you with the two extremely important things: guidance and savings. They will be delighted to help you find the money need to pay for college.

The College Answer Service. First, they have a toll free hotline where you can speak to a financial aid expert who will answer your questions dealing with paying for college, loans, aid packages, advice on finacial aid applications, deadlines, and lots more. You will also learn how to save hundreds with the lowest cost student loans available. Loans with

Sallie Mae can cost a lot less to pay back. Call them Monday through Friday between the hours of 9am to 9pm EST at:
1-800-891-4599.
Sallie Mae also has a number of helpful booklets including *Paying For College* and *Borrowing For College* .
Paying For College is a comprehensive guide-book which provides thorough advice on planning for a college education. The book addresses key financial aid terms, formulas for calculating the Expected Family Contribution, an overview of the federal student loan program and a summary of loan repayment programs ...many of which reward students for on-time payment.
Borrowing For College helps students and their parents choose low-cost student loan lenders in their area. To get free copies call:
1-800-806-3681

www.salliemae.com
One visit to their web site and you will see just how valuable it is. You will be able to do an free online search for scholarship money available from over 300,000 sources. Plus you can e-mail your financial aid questions and get quick advice from experts. The way it works is that when you visit their site you can fill out a questionaire that they will forward to a company called EDTECH. This company will process your questionaire and will send you a list of scholarships that you may qualify for. The best part of all is that there is no charge for any of this scholarship search information.

www.srnexpress.com/
Another great web site to search for free money for college is Scholarship Resource NetworkExpress. This site contains a database of over 8,000 programs where they have over 150,000 awards. You'll also find information about loan forgiveness programs for college graduates who need alternatives for repayment.

FINDING COLLEGE AID
www.fastweb.com
Looking for money to pay for college? This web site is one of the best places to start. It contains a search

engine with information on some 600,000 scholarships sources of money for college.

www.finaid.org
Contains descriptions of different types of college loans, grants and access to scholarships with a FastWEB link plus forms that will help you estimate your financial needs.

www.theoldschool.org
The Financial Aid Resource Center website provides information on the basics of financial aid, access to federal, state and general aid sources, and links to college and university financial aid home pages.

MAKING COLLEGE COUNT
www.makingcollegecount.com
This site offers advice on where to find scholarships, information on college counseling programs and the hottest professional fields for college students to consider.

STUDENT LOANS & GRANTS
If you're a college student or plan to be one and are short of money to continue your education, be sure to get a free copy of *Funding Your Education* and *The Student Guide.* They are the most comprehensive resources of student financial aid from the U.S. Department of Education. It covers major aid programs including Pell Grants, Stafford Loans and PLUS loans. Write:
THE U.S. DEPARTMENT OF EDUCATION,
**400 MARYLAND AVE. S.W. ROOM 2097
WASHINGTON. D.C. 20202**
CALL THEIR INFORMATION HOTLINE: **1-800-4-FED-AID**

Also, for information on Federal student aid backed by the U.S. Government, be sure to visit the Department of Education's web site at:
www.ed.gov

COLLEGE PLANNING
T. Rowe Price's College Planning Guide helps parents project what a college education may cost for their young children. It's absolutely free. Call:
1-800-225-5132

FINANCIAL AID
Financial Aid from the U.S. Department of Education: Grants, Loans and Work-Study. Student guide to obtaining federal money lists sources, guidelines for eligibility, application procedures, deadlines, phone numbers, and more. It's free from:
CONSUMER INFORMATION CENTER
DEPT 506x
PUEBLO, CO 81009

MEETING COLLEGE COSTS
With the costs of going to college spiraling out of sight many students are not able to attend college without financial assistance. This guide can help you learn whether you're eligible for student aid. Write to:
COLLEGE BOARD PUBLICATIONS
"BIBLIOGRAPHY OF FINANCIAL AID"
45 COLUMBUS AVE.
NEW YORK, NY 10023

COMPARING COLLEGE COSTS
Computer users can quickly compare the cost of more than 1500 public and private colleges and get an estimate of what it will cost to attend. When you call, ask for *College Savings Plus,* a free computer disk available from John Hancock Mutual Life Insurance Co. After you ask for the free computer disk, a John Hancock agent will likely call to ask if you want help devising a savings plan. Call:
1-800-633-1809

PAYING FOR COLLEGE
With the cost of going to college skyrocketing every year, you may be wondering how to pay for your education. *Meeting College Costs* will help you with all the questions you have about paying for your college education. Ask for *Meeting College Costs* free from:
THE COLLEGE BOARD
45 COLUMBUS AVE.
NEW YORK, NY 10023-6992

SELECTING THE RIGHT COLLEGE

Picking the right college is one of the most important decisions a teen must make. To help you make an intelligent choice of the college that best suits your needs, interests and budget, State Farm Insurance has an excellent guide for you. This guide is nearly 300 pages long and is produced by U.S. News and World Report. In it you will find valuable information on over 1,400 universities and colleges about tuition, room and board, financial aid, entrance requirements and lots more. For your copy, call State Farm:

1-888-733-8368

Or visit them on the internet at:

www.statefarm.com

JOB SEARCH

If you are thinking about or seriously looking for a job, this report on *How to Have a Successful Job Search.* is a must for you. This valuable report will provide you with information critical to you and your job search. The author, Kay La Rocca is a professional resume writer and expert on what's out there. Ask for *How to Have A Successful Job Search.* Send a long SASE to:

KL PUBLICATIONS
4003 FOREST DR.
ALQUIPPA, PA 15001

FINDING THE RIGHT JOB

If you're confused about what career direction to go in, get a copy of *Tips For Finding The Right Job.* It will help you evaluate your interests and skills. Write to:

EMPLOYMENT & TRAINING
USDL, 200 CONSTITUTION AVE NW, ROOM N4700
WASHINGTON, DC 20210

Looking Good

LEG TALK

Has this ever happened to you: you're down to your last pair of stockings and late for an important meeting when, for no apparent reason, the stockings 'run'? Would you like to find out why this happens and what you can do about it? Write for your free copy of *Sheer Facts About Hosiery.*

THE HOSIERY ASSOCIATION
3623 LATROBE DRIVE SUITE **130**
CHARLOTTE, **NC 28211**
www.nahm.com

KEEP IT CLEAN

The makers of Moisturel Products would like to show you just how good their skin cleansers and lotions are. If you drop them a card they will send you a *$1.00 discount coupon* good on your next purchase of Moisturel products. Write to:

WESTWOOD PHARMACEUTICALS
468 DEWITT ST.
BUFFALO, **NY 14213**

WARDROBE PLANNING FOR WOMEN

How should you dress for work? When is casual attire appropriate and when is it not? The Lee Company has a free wardrobe guide that will help you answer these questions. The guide presents 10 clothing selections that you can mix and match to wear anywhere. It will not only help you put together a basic wardrobe, but will also recommend accessories that will take your daytime into evening and weekday into weekend wear. A must for every woman. To get your free copy of *Ten Easy Pieces,* call:

1-800-4-LEE-FIT

ASK THE HAIR COLORING EXPERTS

Are you thinking of changing your hair color? Having trouble finding the right shade? Can't cover that problem gray? The experts at Clairol have a toll-free hotline you can call for answers to all your hair coloring questions. Their color consultants will also provide you with helpful tips that will help you look your very best. Call them Monday-Friday 8:30am-8:30pm or Saturday 9am-6pm EST at: **1-800-223-5800.**
You can also visit Clairol website on the Internet at: www.clairol.com

HAIR CARE GUIDANCE & MORE

If you would like advice on how to manage your hair, how to color it or just how to keep it looking good, L'Oreal has the answers for you. Next time you can't decide which shampoo or conditioner is best for your hair type, call the toll-free L'Oreal Guideline Monday-Friday, 10am-7pm EST at: **1-800-631-7358**
Or you can write to them at:
L'OREAL CONSUMER AFFAIRS
PO BOX 98
WESTFIELD, NJ 07091
WWW.LOREALUSA.COM

BEAUTY IS SKIN DEEP

Has anyone ever told you, "you are what you eat." The basics of looking good and feeling good, start with healthy eating habits. The American Dietetic Association is making a concerted effort to get us back on a healthy eating track. They have a toll-free phone line you can call weekdays for more information on healthy eating and a referral service to local dietician. Call the Consumer Nutrition HotLine toll-free at: **1-800-366-1655**
OR VISIT THEIR WEB SITE AT:
WWW.EATRIGHT.ORG

Conservation

TROUT RESTOCKING AID

If you would like to restock your lake or
pond, contact the Federal Hatcheries first.
They offer free assistance in your re-
stocking plans. If their production is
sufficient, they may be able to supply
the trout you need. They also have an
interesting booklet you might want,
*Endangered & Threatened Wildlife
and Plants*. Request it by title when
you write to:
U.S. DEPARTMENT OF THE INTERIOR
FISH & WILDLIFE SERVICE
WASHINGTON, DC 20240

INVITE BIRDS TO YOUR HOME

This large colorful poster-like guide will show you
how to *Invite Birds To Your Home*. It tells how to
attract birds with proper tree plantings that spe-
cific species prefer. You also might want to ask for
Your Hometown, Clean Water Town. For your free
copy write:
SOIL CONSERVATION SERVICE
U.S.D.A.
BOX 2890
WASHINGTON, DC 20013

FOREST CONSERVATION

The book you're reading right now and the lumber
in the house in which you live are just two of the
many products we take for granted that come from
our nation's forests. It is essential that we take care
to preserve and renew our forests. The U.S. Forest
Service has a booklet you will want to have: *Making Paper From Trees* shows how a tree goes from
the forest and ends up as paper. Send a card to:
FOREST SERVICE
U.S. DEPT. OF AGRICULTURE
BOX 2417
WASHINGTON, DC 20013

Computers

PC & MAC CONNECTION

If you are looking for the best deals around in computers, software and accessories some of the best prices you will find are from mail order companies. Even if you decide to buy from a local store, calling mail order companies will allow you to comparison shop to get the lowest price. Each of the companies listed here have been in business for a number of years and have an excellent reputation for customer satisfaction. When you call ask for their latest catalog which will be full of important information to all you to make an intelligent buying decision. Most have a 24 hour customer service line and your orders arrive promptly, often the very next day

PC CONNECTION: **1-800-800-1111**
MAC CONNECTION: **1-800-800-0002**
MacWAREHOUSE: **1-800 255-6227**
CDW: **1-800-328-2261**
MacZONE: **1-800-248-0800**
PC ZONE: **1-800-258-2088**
TIGER DIRECT: **1-800-888-4437**
MacMALL: **1-800-222-2808**
MICROCENTER ONLINE: **1-800-634-3478**
DELL: **1-800-545-3771**

APPLE ASSISTANCE

If you own a Macintosh or are thinking of buying one and have questions you need answered, there's a toll-free number you can call for help.

APPLE HELP LINE: **1-800-SOS-APPL**
OR VISIT THEIR WEB SITE:
WWW.APPLE.COM

COMPUTER SUPPLY CATALOG

If you or your company owns a computer you will want to get a copy of the *Global Computer Supplies Catalog.* This full color catalog lists thousands of computer-related products of all types. Drop a postcard to:

GLOBAL COMPUTER SUPPLIES
11 HARBOR PARK DRIVE
PORT WASHINGTON, NY 11050
OR CALL: 1-800-8-GLOBAL
(THAT'S 1-800-845-6225)
WWW.GLOBALCOMPUTER.COM

THE WORLD AT YOUR FINGER TIP

One of the major advantages of owning a computer is that you can have instant access to people and sources of information that may be thousands of miles from you. In an instant you can surf the Internet with thousands of fascinating web sites. To get started with free software and in many cases with free online trials, call these toll-free numbers:

AMERICA ONLINE: 1-800-827-6364
COMPUSERVE: 1-800-848-8199
MICROSOFT NETWORK: 1-800-386-5550
EARTHLINK: 1-800-890-6356

FREE SOFTWARE STUDENT SPECIAL

Professor Weissman will send you a free educational computer disc for PC's and compatibles. He has great programs including algebra, trigonometry, precalculus, statistics and math for nursing. All you have to do is include $2.00 postage & handling (or a SASE requesting more information) to:

PROFESSOR WEISSMAN'S SOFTWARE
246 CRAFTON AVE.
STATEN ISLAND, NY 10314

FREE COMPUTER SUPPLIES

Right now there's intense competition going on between several nationwide computer retailers. To bring you into their store, each of them offers free computer supplies with a full rebate. For example in the last several weeks we have received several hundred computer diskettes, surge protectors, laser paper, a computer mouse, and other computer related items all of which came with a 100% rebate. Hundreds of dollars in supplies absolutely free! Check your local newspapers (especially the weekend editions) for full page ads and inserts for CompUSA, Circuit City, Staples and other nationwide chain stores.

FREE SCREEN SAVERS

Screen savers can turn a dull gray computer screen into a beautiful work of art. For hundreds of free screen savers, visit the following web sites:
www.freesaver.com
www.cinemadesktopthemes.com
www.topdesktop.com

FREE ON THE INTERNET

Thousands of pieces of software are available absolutely free on the Internet. If you have a computer and a modem, accessing the Internet is a simple and easy way to open up a whole new world. Among other things, you will find 'freeware', 'shareware' and free computer application upgrades waiting for you to download into your computer. You will also find full text of hundreds of useful government booklets and reports on a host of fascinating subjects all of which you can download free. Check the next section in this book for lots more free things on the Internet.

Free Things, Great Bargains & More On The Internet

Although only a few years old, the most revolutionary change of this century in the way we live, shop, and exchange information has been the advent of the Internet. The Internet has placed the entire world just a mouse click away from you. You can now shop for amazing bargains anywhere in the world. You can empty your attic of old treasures you no longer need (and pick up some extra cash) by selling them at an online auction site. But best of all for all lovers of free things, you can now stuff your mailbox with hundreds of terrific samples and trial offers...all absolutely free and all without ever leaving the comfort of your home.

The day is rapidly approaching when access to the Internet will be as common and as necessary as having a phone. But today although over 90 million people have access to the Internet, what can you do if you don't have a computer yet? Does this mean you have to miss out on all the wonders you'll find on the Internet? Fortunately the answer is "no". You have several options.

The simplest option is to use the computer you'll find at your local library. Virtually all libraries now have computers you can use and a librarian who is happy to show you how to log on to the 'net'. Next, since the prices of computers and Internet access has come way down (and will likely continue to drop), now might be the time to consider taking the plunge and getting a home computer. In fact if you shop around, you'll find numerous offers that allow you to get a computer for free or nearly free just by signing up for Internet access. In any event, no matter what direction you choose, be sure to get some form of Internet access...*soon*.

Now let's take a look at the best the Internet offers for lovers of free things and for bargain shoppers. First lets look at the best sites for those who love getting something for nothing.

www.totallyfreestuff.com
At this site they are trying to build the most comprehensive list of 'free stuff' on the Internet. Just checking through their 29 categories, you'll find just about everything from pet food to CD's, audio tapes, stickers and posters of all types, and product samples like popcorn, milk substitute, Alka Seltzer, nasal strips, Papers, skin care products, pedicure kit...to mention just a few. A great place to visit for all lovers of free things.

www.4free.net
Free health products, free games, free pet stuff and

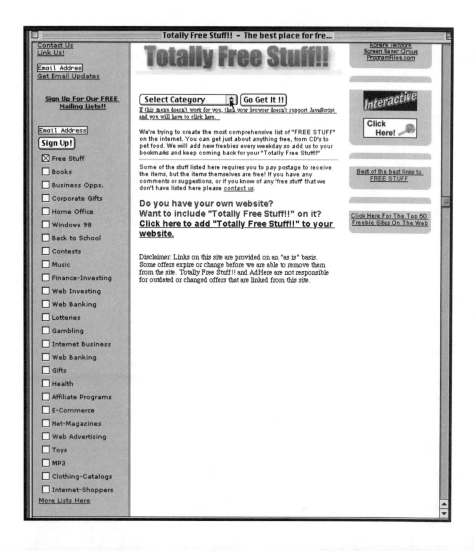

free samples are just a few of the 47 different categories of free things that you'll find at this web site. You can even sign up for news and special offers geared to your interests with hundreds of subjects to choose from.

www.weeklyfreebie.com

Each week you'll find an updated list of free things in categories list pets, food, travel, catalogs, computers and coupons. This site features links to other Internet sites that give away free things. For example, if you click on 'coupons' you are then given a wide choice of categories such as clothing, health & beauty and food. Let's say you then click on 'food', you'll discover links to web sites for Mrs. Fields cookies, I Can't Believe It's Not Butter and Ragu to mention just a few. At each site you'll find information on getting free coupons for various products.

www.freeshop.com

You'll find a hundreds of free and trial offers here at the freeshop.com site. There are dozens of categories to choose from. Start by clicking on the areas of greatest interest to you and you will be presented with an array of products and offers to pick from. Just as an example, there are over 500 magazine offers, over 300 offers for kids & family and more than 100 software offers to choose from...and that's just the beginning. Note that many of the offers are trial offers where you may receive a free issue of a magazine. If you don't want to continue your subscription after you have looked over the free issue, you simply cancel, keep the issue and you owe nothing.

www.freemania.com

Check at the freemania.com web site for the five new free things they add each day plus the hottest and most valuable freebies of the week. Select from listings for apparel, health freebies, cosmetics, food samples and games to mention a few. You'll also find links to over 300 free catalogs so your mailbox will always be filled to overflowing.

www.nojunkfree.com

At this site they believe in bringing you the best freebies on the web. They promise to always filter out all of the stuff they consider to be junk. They offer you a free bi-weekly newsletter filled with free stuff. The web master at this site not only describes the free things you'll receive but also ranks the listing based on the quality of the items received.

www.freethings.com

At this site the free things you'll find change from one week to another. As an example of the kinds of freebies you may find, a recent visit to this site revealed freebies that included free games, a Rainbow Kids Baby Hat, and a personalized Auto e-mail newsletter with driving tips and information on auto recalls and repairs. You'll also find 'SellStuff' which is online classifieds where you can buy or sell used all kinds of things.

IMPORTANT NOTE:

Many of the offers you'll find at the various free things sites are what are called 'trial offers'. With a trial offer you have a certain amount of time to preview the product or publication. After that time, you can keep the product and pay for it or cancel your order and owe nothing. For example, at www.smartbiz.com/cd you will receive a free issue of Catholic Digest filled with spiritually uplifting and inspirational articles plus wholesome activities for the entire family. That issue is yours to keep with no obligation to continue with a paid subscription. But if you do decide to continue with a subscription to Catholic Digest you'll also receive a free book, *All About Angels*. That's a trial offer.

Just be wary if you are asked to submit your credit card number. With this type of offer your credit card will be charged automatically if you don't cancel within the time allowed (usually 30 days). Unless you are sure you will contact them if you decide not to continue, our advice would be to avoid any offer where you are asked to submit your credit card number to get your freebie.

FREE MUSICAL GREETING CARD

Yahoo! Greetings is one of the coolest sites on the Internet today. Here you can e-mail anyone you choose an animated electronic

greeting card personalized with your name and message. There are dozens of delightful cards for all occasions to choose from...birthdays, sympathy, weddings and anniversaries plus lots more. Once you've selected the card and personalized it with your message, you then e-mail to the person you are sending it to. Instantly it pops into their e-mail waiting for them to open. When they do open it, they will find a beautifully drawn card with figures that do a little dance to music. You're sure to love this site...and so will the people you send the cards to.
http://greetings.yahoo.com

SAVING MONEY WITH 'ONLINE' COUPONS

If you enjoy saving money using coupons, you gonna love this site. In fact you'll think you've died and gone to coupon heaven because you'll find virtually every type of coupon imaginable. First go to this site and just type in your city and state. You'll be transported to a site that has coupons for everything you can imagine ... hair salons, restaurants, auto repair, dry cleaning, landscaping... you name it, you'll find it here. Check it out.
www.hotcoupons.com

INSTANT COUPON SAVINGS

How would you like to join the more than 3 million smart shoppers who have enrolled in coolsavings.com? Once you fill out a short form online you will be given a free enrollment that will entitle you to receive coupons of your choice downloaded right into your computer and printed out on your own printer. You can start saving money immediately rather than have to wait for your coupons to arrive by mail.
www.coolsavings.com

CATALOG SHOPPING AT HOME

In addition to using retail stores and the Internet to shop, many people enjoy shopping from mail order catalogs. If that describes you, check out the following Internet sites where you find hundreds of free catalogs waiting for you.

www.shopathome.com

Here you'll find more than 300 catalogs to choose from featuring everything from tasty steaks to tasteful apparel. Simply click on the catalogs you would like to receive and they'll be sent to you.

www.catalogsavings.com

This site is almost overwhelming in scope. While the individual catalogs are not listed, at any one time up to 10,000 catalogs are available. The way it works is that you select from a list of over 400 topics. Once you click on a topic and fill in your name & address, you will receive any number of catalogs that feature products that you've indicated an interest in.

www.2000freebies.com

Although at this site you again select only categories of products you're interested in and not individual catalogs, you will see what free catalogs you're ordering. Choose from a long list of categories including automotive, toys, audio, video, books, fashion and crafts to mention a few.

GET RID OF SPAM

When you sign up for all kinds of free things online, in addition to receiving your free gifts from the company you request them from, you may also receive 'junk mail' or junk e-mail (known as 'spam') once your name has been sold to other companies. You may find the mountain of mail interesting but in case you don't, you can request that your name be removed from these lists. This service is free when you contact Ultimate Resource web site at:
www.ultimateresourcesite.com

LOWER INTEREST RATE ON LOANS

If you have to borrow money for any purpose... mortgage, debt consolidation, credit card repayment, car loan...you know how expensive the interest can be especially if you have to finance a large amount payable over several years. Until recently you were at the mercy of your local bank or lending institution and the rates they charged. Now with the Internet no matter where you live you can actually shop the entire nation for the lowest interest rate at lendingtree.com

LendingTree is the only online loan marketplace where lenders compete for your business. And since they are competing for your business, you will find great rates and terms. You then choose the loan that's best for you. You're likely to find this the easiest way to get a loan you've ever experienced. They also have loan calculators that will help you determine the amount to borrow and estimate your monthly payments. Check them out at:
www.lendingtree.com

CHEAP THREADS ON THE WEB

Bargain hunters who don't want to run all over the place to check out the outlet malls can now check these bargains out on the web:
www.bluefly.com:
Discounts up to 75% Shoes, clothes, accessories, housewares. You type in your size and favorite designer and it will show you items that match.

www.outletmall.com
Men's and women's shoes, clothes and beauty products. The longer the merchandise is on the site the lower the price drops.

www.discountshopper.com
Housewares, electronics, luggage, jewelry, toys, and apparel at discount prices.

AIR FARE BARGAINS

www.priceline.com
Priceline has come up with a novel way of saving you money on your next trip. The way it works is that Priceline gets listings of unsold airline seats and unbooked hotel rooms. Using the Internet you then can name the price you want to pay for the airline ticket or the hotel room. If your price is ac-

ceptable you are then booked and if not they will suggest a price that should get you the space you're looking for. The reason it works so well is that airlines and hotels would rather accept a lower price than have their space go unused and get nothing. At this site you will also find attractive rates on home mortgages and automobiles.

www.jetblue.com

AtJetBlue's web site you'll find web-only specials. These special fares are updated regularly and include specials on hotels and rental cars as well as on their air fares.

www.aa.com

At American Airlines the Internet specials can be viewed online at their web site. If you see a low fare that you want, act quickly because most are quickly snapped up.

my.netscape.com

MyNetscape offers free Web pages which include an airfare tracking service. Once you enter your favorite destinations, the prices are automatically updated when you return to your page.

www.smarterliving.com

At the Smarter Living Web site users can sign up for a free weekly e-mail that summarizes special offers from 20 airlines.

www.Travelocity.com
www.Orbitz.com
www.Hotwire.com
www.cheaptickets.com

Checking out the fares at these web sites will help you find the lowest airfares. So before you travel do some comparison shopping for airfares on these web sites. You can wind up saving hundreds of dollars.

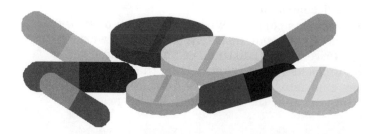

SAVE ON DRUGS & VITAMINS

www.medications-online.com
Medications Online is your Internet neighborhood pharmacist, no matter where you live. With the help of the Internet, you can now ask questions and have a more personal relationship with your pharmacist. You will get lower price quotes as well as faster and better service. So next time you need the best price, on prescription drugs, check them out.

www.drugstore.com
Here's a great way to shop for all your health needs, as well as beauty products and information. It's a great way to shop for your next prescription without having to wait on line at the pharmacy. They focus on helping you make your life easier by shopping online.

BUY OR LEASE YOUR NEXT CAR?

How can you get the lowest price on your next car? Should you buy your car or lease it? If you aren't sure about the advantages and disadvantages, next time you look for a car, or you are looking for the best deals there are several sites to check out.

To find the Kelly Blue Book, where you can get information on how much the dealer pays for a car:
www.kbb.com

For car price quotes and financing rates:
www.carwizard.com

For terrific lease deals:
www.intellichoice.com

For the lowest prices on your next car :
www.autobytel.com

If you're interested in getting a good deal on a used car, try:
www.autoconnect.com

To get new car reviews, check prices and compare financing and insurance quotes, go to:
www.carprices.com

BARGAIN SHOPPING WITH ONLINE AUCTIONS

Online auctions are the hottest rage on the Internet today. If you love the challenge and excitement of competing for a super bargain, you must check out the online auction sites. You can do a search through their enormous databases which at any one time may have several million different items being auctioned by individuals throughout the country. You will find everything under the sun from outboard motors to jewelry to furbys and antiques. One thing you should keep in mind as you start placing your bids for items you want is to be careful not to get so caught up in the process that you wind up bidding more for an item than it is worth just so you will 'win' the bidding.

eBay is the world's largest online auction site. It was the first to initiate the person-to-person auction format. The site is easy to use because the seller gets plenty of space to display and describe the item

they are auctioning. To make it more comfortable for customers to trade online, eBay offers free insurance through Lloyds of London. Visit them at:
www.ebay.com

Another attractive auction site to check out is ubid. Where eBay focuses mainly on individuals who want to sell items they no longer want, ubid focuses on businesses that want to dispose of surplus inventory, refurbished products and small lots. Check it out, you could come across a great deal:
www.ubid.com

At Yahoo! Auction you you'll find just about everything you can imagine listed within the hundreds of categories of items you can bid on. They will even keep track of all of the open auctions you are currently bidding on. Visit their site at:
http://auction.yahoo.com

ONLINE SURPLUS LIQUIDATIONS
If you are looking for great buys on virtually anything, be sure to check out half.com. This site specializes in selling surplus inventories that companies have... at drastically reduced prices. On this site you will find everything from books to music CDs to computers at savings of up to 50% or even more.
www.half.com

WIN UP TO $10 MILLION AT THIS SITE

An Internet company called iWon has come up with a unique way of attracting people to its web site...they have a sweepstakes where they give away $10,000 each day and $10 million once a year. The way it works is that when you go to their site, you have a variety of things you can do...read the news, buy anything from autos to mortgages or search the Internet for other sites you may be interested in. But each time you use iWon to go to a site you earn points. The more sites you visit, the more entries you earn. These entries then automatically enter you in a lottery where you have a chance at winning big cash prizes. All this is free just for using their site. To learn more and to earn entry into their lottery, visit their web site at:
www.iwon.com

WOMEN AND BUSINESS

The World Wide Web has become a rich (and free) resource for women who plan to become their own boss or want to get some direction in personal financial planning. Here are some sites that provide women with free financial information and self-owned business insights.

www.wife.org
This site contains information on a wide range of financial and investing topics specifically for woman of all ages.

www.digital-women.com
Digital Woman provides information and tips for women who own or would like to run their own businesses.

www.ivillage.com
ivillage.com features information and articles of interest to women incoluding beauty, diet and fitness tips, recipes and a lot more.

FREE SEARCH SITES ON THE INTERNET

The best thing about the Internet is that it contains just about anything you'd ever want to find. The worst thing about the Internet is that it's often almost impossible to find just what you want. The problem is...without searching through thousands of sites, how do you find the specific information you need or at least narrow the search down to a manageable number? Fortunately, the Internet has a number of excellent search engines that allow you type in a sentence in plain English and then a flash it will search through its database of millions of web sites and come back to you with a list of likely places for you to check out. And all this hard work is done for you...absolutely free.

So the next time you want to find the research a video camera you are thinking of buying or locate the lowest price on your car insurance, let these search engines do all the leg work for you...you'll be amazed at how good they are:

www.altavista.com
www.pricegrabber.com
www.google.com
www.dogpile.com
www.askjeeves.co

FREE INTERNET ACCESS

If you are paying too much for your internet access, maybe you should check out Juno.com and NetZero.com. These two web 'portals' will give you an entry point to surf the web. They both feature a totally free option for those who only use the internet infrequently. They also offer a low priced option (that's less than half the price of other portals) that will give you unlimited access 24 hours a day, 7 days a week. Check out each at:

www.juno.com
www.netzero.com

For Sports Fans

Do you love sports? How would you like to receive photos of your favorite teams? Most sports clubs have all kinds of freebies for their loyal fans. These neat freebies often include team photos, souvenir brochures, stickers, fan club information, playing schedules, catalogs and lots more. All you have to do is write to your favorite sports teams at the addresses in this book. Tell them you're a loyal fan and ask them for a "fan package."

Even though it's not always necessary, it's always nice idea to send a long self-addressed-stamped envelope with your name & address written in so they can return your freebie right in your own envelope.

Also, if you have a favorite player on the team, write his name on the envelope.

Sometimes it takes a while to get an answer since most teams are absolutely flooded with mail. Just be patient and you will hear from them.

HOCKEY
National Hockey League One
International Blvd.
Rexdale, Ontario
Canada M9W 6H3
www.nhl.com

EASTERN CONFERENCE

Atlanta Thrashers Hockey Club
Atlanta, GA 30348-5366
www.atlantathrashers.com

Boston Bruins
One FleetCenter Ste. 250
Boston, MA 02fi4-1303
www.bostonbruins.com

Buffalo Sabres
Marine Midland Arena
One Seymore H. Knox III Plaza
Buffalo, NY 14203
www.sabres.com

Carolina Hurricanes Hockey Club
Entertainment & Sports Arena
1400 Edwards Mill Rd.
Raleigh, NC 27607
www.caneshockey.com

Florida Panthers Hockey Club
One Panthers Pkwy.
Sunrise, FL 33323
www.floridapanthers.com

Montreal Canadiens
Molson Centre
1280 de la Gauchetiere St. W
Montreal, Quebec
Canada H3B 5E8
www.canadiens.com

New Jersey Devils
Continental Airlines Arena
50 Route 120 North
E. Rutherford, NJ 07073
www.newjerseydevils.com

New York Islanders
Nassau Veterans Memorial Coliseum
1255 Hempstead Tnpk.
Uniondale, NY 11553
www.newyorkislanders.com

New York Rangers
Madison Square Garden
Two Pennsylvania Plaza, 14th flr.
New York, NY 10121
www.newyorkrangers.com

Ottawa Senators Hockey Club
Corel Centre
1000 Palladium Dr.
Kanata, Ontario
Canada K2V 1A5
www.ottawasenators.com

Philadelphia Flyers
First Union Center
3601 S. Broad St.
Philadelphia, PA 19148
www.philadelphiaflyers.com

Pittsburgh Penguins
Mellon Arena
66 Mario Lemieux Pl.
Pittsburgh, PA 15219
www.pittsburghpenguins.com

Tampa Bay Lightning
Ice Palace Arena
401 Channelside Dr.
Tampa, FL 33602
www.tampabaylightning.com

Toronto Maple Leafs
Air Canada Centre
40 Bay St.
Toronto, Ontario
Canada M5J 2X2
www.mapleleafs.com

Washington Capitals
Market Square North
401 Nitnth St. NW, Suite 750
Washington, DC 20004
www.washingtoncaps.com

WESTERN CONFERENCE

Anaheim Mighty Ducks
Arrowhead Pond of Anaheim
2695 Katella Ave.
Anaheim, CA 92806
www.mightyducks.com

Calgary Flames
Pengrowth Saddledome
PO Box 1540, Station M
Calgary, Alberta
Canada T2P 3B9
www.calgaryflames.com

Chicago Blackhawks
United Center
1901 W. Madison St.
Chicago, IL 60612
www.chicagoblackhawks.com

Colorado Avalanche
Pepsi Center
1000 Chopper Cir.
Denver, CO 80204
www.coloradoavalanche.com

Columbus Blue Jackets
Nationwide Arena
200 W. Nationwide Blvd.
Suite Level
Columbus, OH 43125
www.bluejackets.com

Dallas Stars
Dr. Pepper StarCenter-Valley Ranch
211 Cowboys Pkwy.
Irving, TX 75063
www.dallasstars.com

Detroit Red Wings
Joe Louis Arena
600 Civic Center Dr.
Detroit, MI 48226
www.detroitredwings.com

Edmonton Oilers
Skyreach Centre
11230 110 St.
Edmonton, Alberta
Canada T5G H7
www.edmontonoilers.com

Los Angeles Kings
Staples Center
1111 S. Figueroa St.
Los Angeles, CA 90015
www.lakings.com

Minnesota Wild
317 Washington St.
St. Paul, MN 55102
www.wild.com

Nashville Predators
501 Broadway
Nashville, TN 37203
www.nashvillepredators.com

Phoenix Coyotes
Alltel Ice Den
9375 E. Bell Rd.
Scottsdale, AZ 85260
www.phoenixcoyotes.com

San Jose Sharks
525 W. Santa Clara St.
San Jose, CA 95113
www.sjsharks.com

St. Louis Blues
Savvis Center
1401 Clark Ave.
St. Louis, MO 03103-2709
www.stlouisblues.com

Vancouver Canucks
General Motors Place
800 Griffiths Way
Vancouver, BC
Canada V6B 6G1
www.canucks.com

BASKETBALL

Atlanta Hawks
One CNN Center
Ste. 405
Atlanta, GA 30303
www.nba.com/hawks

Boston Celtics
FleetCenter
151 Merrimac St., 5th flr.
Boston, MA 02114
www.nba.com/celtics

Chicago Bulls
United Center
1901 W. Madison St.
Chicago, IL 60612-2459
www.nba.com/bulls

Cleveland Cavaliers
One Center Court
Cleveland, OH 44115
www.nba.com/cavs

Dallas Mavericks
American Airlines Center
2500 Victory Ave.
Dallas, TX 75201
www.nba.com/mavericks

Denver Nuggets
PO Box 4568
1635 Clay St.
Denver, CO 80204
www.nba.com/nuggets

Detroit Pistons
Palace of Auburn Hills
Two Championship Dr.
Auburn Hills, MI 48326
www.nba.com/pistons

Golden State Warriors
1011 Broadway, 20th flr.
Oakland, CA 94607
www.nba.com/warriors

Houston Rockets
Two Greenway Plaza, Ste. 400
Houston, TX 77046
www.nba.com/rockets

Indiana Pacers
125 S. Pennsylvania St.
Indianapolis, IN 46204
www.nba.com/pacers

Los Angeles Clippers
Staples Center
1111 S. Figueroa St.
Los Angeles, CA 90015
www.nba.com/clippers

Los Angeles Lakers
Staples Center
I1111 S. Figueroa St.
Los Angeles, CA 90015
www.nba.com/lakers

Memphis Grizzlies
175 Toyota Pl., Ste. 150
Memphis, TN 38103
www.Grizzlies.com

Miami Heat
American Airlines Arena
601 Biscayne Blvd.
Miami, FL 33132
www.nba.com/heat

Milwaukee Bucks
Bradley Center
1001 N. Fourth St.
Milwaukee, WI 53203
www.nba.com/bucks

Minnesota Timberwolves
600 First Ave. N
Minneapolis, MN 55403
www.nba.com/timberwolves

New Jersey Nets
390 Murray Hill Pkwy.
E. Rutherford, NJ 07073
www.nba.com/nets

New Orleans Hornets
1501 Girod St.
New Orleans, LA 70113
www.neworleans.nba.com/
hornets

New York Knicks
Madison Square Garden
Two Pennsylvania Plaza
New York, NY 10121
www. nba.com/knicks

Orlando Magic
TD Waterhouse Centre
One Magic Pl.
600 West Ameila
Orlando, FL 32802
www.nba.com/magic

Philadelphia '76ers
First Union Center
3601 S. Broad St.
Philadelphia, PA 19148
www.nba.com/sixers

Phoenix Suns
America West Arena
201 E. Jefferson St.
Phoenix, AZ 85004
www.nba.com/suns

Portland Trail Blazers
One Center Court, Ste. 200
Portland, OR 97201
www.nba.com/blazers

Sacramento Kings
Arco Arena
One Sports Pkwy.
Sacramento, CA 95834
www.nba.com/kings

San Antonio Spurs
100 Montana
San Antonio, TX 78203
www.nba.com/spurs

Seattle Sonics & Storm
351 Elliott Ave. W., Ste. 500
Seattle, WA 98119
www.nba.com/sonics

Toronto Raptors
Air Canada Centre
40 Bay St.
Toronto, Ontario
Canada M5J 2X2
www.nba.com/raptors

Utah Jazz
Delta Center
301 W. South Temple
Salt Lake City, UT 84101
www.nba.com/jazz

Washington Wizards
MCI Center
601 F Street NW
Washington, DC 20004
www.nba.com/wizards

FOOTBALL

National Football League
280 Park Ave.
New York, NY 10017
www.nfl.com

AMERICAN CONFERENCE

Baltimore Ravens
11001 Owings Mills Blvd.
Owings Mills, MD 21117
www.ravenszone.net

Buffalo Bills
One Bills Dr.
Orchard Park, NY 14127
www.buffalobills.com

Cincinnati Bengals
One Paul Brown Stadium
Cincinnati, OH 45202
www.bengals.com

Cleveland Browns
80 First Ave.
Cleveland, OH 44146
www.clevelandbrowns.com

Denver Broncos
Mile High Stadium
1900 Eliot St.
Denver, CO 80204-1721
www.denverbroncos.com

Houston Texans
711 Louisiana, 33rd flr.
Houston, TX 77002-2716
www.houstontexans.com

Indianapolis Colts
7001 W. 56 St.
Indianapolis, IN 46254
www.colts.com

Jacksonville Jaguars
One ALLTEL Stadium Pl.
Jacksonville, FL 32202
www.jaguars.corn

Kansas City Chiefs
One Arrowhead Dr.
Kansas City, MO 64129
www.kcchiefs.com

Miami Dolphins
Pro Player Stadium
2269 NW 199 St.
Miami, FL 33056
www.miamidolphins.com

New England Patriots
60 Washington St.
Foxboro, MA 02035
www.patriots.com

New York Jets
Giants Stadium
East Rutherford, NJ 07073
or
1000 Fulton Ave.
Hempstead, NY 11550
www.newyorkjets.com/
index2new.php

Oakland Raiders
1220 Harbor Bay Pkwy.
Alameda, CA 94502
www.raiders.com

Pittsburgh Steelers
PO Box 6763
Pittsburgh, PA 15212
www.steelers.com

San Diego Chargers
PO Box 609609
San Diego, CA 92160-9609
www.chargers.com

Tennessee Titans
Baptist Sports Park
460 Great Circle Rd.
Nashville, TN 37228
www.titans.com

NATIONAL CONFERENCE

Arizona Cardinals
8701 S. Hardy Dr.
Phoenix, AZ 85284
www.cardinals.com

Atlanta Falcons
4400 Falcon Pkwy.
Flowery Branch, GA 30542
www.atlantafalcons.com

Carolina Panthers
Ericsson Stadium
800 S. Mint St.
Charlotte, NC 28202
www.carolinapanthers.com

Chicago Bears
Halas Hall
1000 Football Dr.
Lake Forest, IL 60045
ww.chicagobears.com

Dallas Cowboys
Texas Stadium
2401 East Airport Freeway
Irving, TX 75063
www.dallascowboys.com

Detroit Lions
1200 Featherstone Rd.
Pontiac, MI 48342
www.detroitlions.com

Green Bay Packers
1265 Lombardi Ave.
Green Bay, WI 54304
www.packers.com

Minnesota Vikings
Winter Park Administrative
Offices
9520 Viking Dr.
Eden Prairie, MN 55344
www.vikings.com

The New Orleans Saints
5800 Airline Dr.
Metairie, LA 70003
www.neworleanssaints.com

New York Football Giants
Giants Stadium
East Rutherford, NJ 07073
www.newyorkgiants.com

Philadelphia Eagles
Veterans Stadium
3501 S. Broad St.
Philadelphia, PA 19148-5201
www.philadelphiaeagles.com

San Francisco 49ers
4949 Centennial Blvd.
Santa Clara, CA 95054
www.sf49ers.com

Seattle Seahawks
11220 N.E. 53 St.
Kirkland, WA 98033
www.seahawks.com

St. Louis Rams
901 North Broadway
St. Louis, MO 63101
www.stlouisrams.com

Tampa Bay Buccaneers
One Buccaneer Pl.
Tampa, FL 33607
www. buccaneers. com

Washington Redskins
21300 Redskin Park Dr.
Ashburn, VA 20147
www.redskins.com

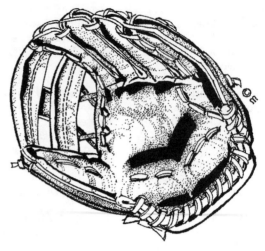

BASEBALL

Major League Baseball
MLB Advanced Media
New York, NY 10011
866-225-6457
www. majorleaguebaseball.com

AMERICAN LEAGUE

Anaheim Angels
angels.mlb.com
2000 Gene Autry Way
Anaheim, CA 92806
www.anaheim.angels.mlb.com

Baltimore Orioles
Oriole Park at Camden Yards
333 W. Camden St.
Baltimore, MD 21201
www.baltimore.orioles.mlb.com

Boston Red Sox
Four Yawkey Way
Boston, MA 02215-3496
www.boston.redsox.mlb.com

Chicago White Sox
333 W. 35 St.
Chicago, IL 60616
www.chicago.whitesox.mlb.com

Cleveland Indians
Jacobs Field
2401 Ontario St.
Cleveland, OH 44115-4003
www.cleveland.indians.mlb.com

Detroit Tigers
Commerce Park
2100 Woodward Ave.
Detroit, MI 48201
www.detroit.tigers.mlb.com

Kansas City Royals
One Royal Way
Kansas City, MO 64129
www.kansascity.royals.mlb.com

Minnesota Twins
Metrodome
34 Kirby Puckett Pl.
Minneapolis, MN 55415
www.minnesota.twins.mlb.com

New York Yankees
Yankee Stadium
161st St. and River Ave.
Bronx, NY 10451
www.newyork.yankees.mlb.com

Oakland Athletics
7677 Oakport St., Ste. 200
Oakland, CA 94621
www.oakland.athletics.mlb.com

Seattle Mariners
SAFECO Field
1250 First Ave. S.
Seattle, WA 98134
www.seattle.mariners.mlb.com

Tampa Bay Devil Rays
Tropicana Field
One Tropicana Dr.
St. Petersburg, FL 33705
www.tampabay.devilrays.mlb.com

Texas Rangers
1000 Ballpark Way, #4oo
Arlington, TX 76011
www.texas.rangers.mlb.com

Toronto Blue Jays
One Blue Jays Way, Ste. 3200
SkyDome
Toronto, Ontario
Canada M5V 1J1
www.toronto.bluejays.mlb.com

NATIONAL LEAGUE

Arizona Diamondbacks
Bank One Ballpark
401 East Jefferson St.
Phoenix, AZ 85001
www.arizona.diamondbacks.mlb.com

Atlanta Braves
755 Hank Aaron Dr.
Atlanta, GA 30315
www.atlanta.braves.mlb.com

Chicago Cubs
Wrigley Field
1060 W. Addison
Chicago, IL 60613
www.chicago.cubs.mlb.com

Cincinnati Reds
100 Cinergy Field
Cincinnati, OH 45202
www.cincinnati.reds.mlb.com

Colorado Rockies
Coors Field
2001 Blake St.
Denver, C0 80205-2000
www.colorado.rockies.mlb.com

Florida Marlins
Pro Player Stadium
2269 Dan Marino Blvd.
Miami, FL 33056
www.florida.marlins.mlb.com

Houston Astros
501 Crawford St.
Houston, TX 77002
www.houston.astros.mlb.com

Los Angeles Dodgers
Dodger Stadium
1000 Elysian Park Ave.
Los Angeles, CA 90012-1199
www.losangeles.dodgers.mlb.com

Milwaukee Brewers
One Brewers Way
Milwaukee, WI 53214-3652
www.milwaukee.brewers.mlb.com

Montreal Expos
4549 Avenue Pierrede Coubertin
Montreal, Quebec
Canada HIV3N7
www.montreal.expos.mlb.com

New York Mets
Shea Stadium
123-01 Roosevelt Ave.
Flushing, NY 11368-1699
www.newyork.mets.mlb.com

Philadelphia Phillies
Veterans Stadium
3501 S. Broad St.
Philadelphia, PA 19148
www.philadelphia.phillies.mlb.com

Pittsburgh Pirates
PNC Park at North Shore
115 Federal St.
Pittsburgh, PA 15212
www.pittsburg.pirates.mlb.com

St. Louis Cardinals
250 Stadium Plaza
St. Louis, MO 63102
www.stlouis.cardinals.mlb.com

San Diego Padres
PO Box 12200
San Diego, CA 92112-2000
www.sandiego.padres.mlb.com

San Francisco Giants
Pacific Bell Park
24 Willie Mays Plaza
San Francisco, CA 94107
www.sanfrancisco.giants.mlb.com

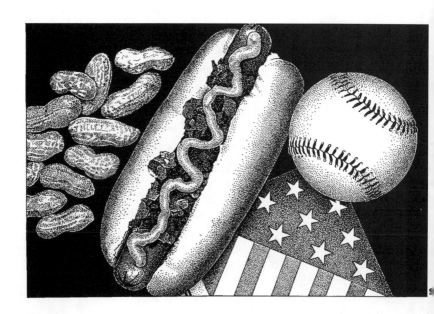

OUTDOOR SPORTS

L. L. Bean, the outdoor sporting specialists for over 70 years, would like to send you a copy of their *catalog*. It features apparel and footwear for the outdoorsman or woman as well as equipment for camping, fishing, hiking and canoeing. Call L.L. Bean at:
1-800-441-5713
www.llbean.com

GETTING IN SHAPE

It's always a great idea to get in shape and stay in shape. Just remember that if you take better care of your body, it will take better care of you. The President's Council on Physical Fitness & Sports has useful information that will help you stay fit. You'll get an introduction to exercise, weight control, physical fitness, sports, running and lots more. Here are a few titles you will want to ask for
• *Pep up Your Life*
• *Exercise & Weight Control*-they go hand in hand.
• *Fitness Fundamentals* - how to develop a personal fitness program
Drop a card to:
THE PRESIDENT'S COUNCIL ON PHYSICAL FITNESS & SPORTS
200 INDEPENDENCE AVE. SW ROOM 738H
WASHINGTON, D.C. 20201
202-690-9000

HOCKEY CARDS

If you are a hockey fan, you'll definitely want to send for this freebie. You will receive 10 free hockey cards. To get your cards, send a SASE and 50¢ to:
DANORS, DEPARTMENT H
5721 FUNSTON STREET BAY 14
HOLLYWOOD, FL 33023

THE OLYMPIC GAMES

"The History of The Olympics" gives you the complete story of the Olympics starting with the earliest recorded game in 776 B.C. and traces the games' history through the present. For your free copy, visit their web site at:
www.olympic-usa.org

99 TIPS FOR FAMILY FITNESS

One of the best ways to stay in shape is by involving the whole family in a fitness progam. In *99 Tips* you'll find a slew of fun fitness activities for kids and parents alike. You'll also find advice from notable athletes like Troy Aikman. Just send a card to:

99 TIPS FOR FAMILY FITNESS
MET-Rx FOUNDATION FOR HEALTH ENHANCEMENT
2112 BUSINESS CENTER DRIVE
IRVINE, CA 92715

LITTLE LEAGUE BASEBALL

Little League Baseball has built character, team play, physical fitness and most importantly—the drive to win—in thousands of youngsters throughout America. If you're involved (or plan to be involved) with the Little League you may want to get a copy of the *Little League Baseball Equipment Supplies catalog*. It's free from:

LITTLE LEAGUE BASEBALL, INC.
P.O. Box 3485
WILLIAMSPORT, PA 17701

BASEBALL EXPRESS

Do you need gear for your baseball team or club? Or, would you like to have a replica jersey from your favorite baseball team? You can receive a free catalog from Baseball Express. For a free copy of this huge catalog, jammed with more than 3,000 different baseball and softball products, call toll-free:

800-9374824

Or just complete the form by clicking on "Request a Catalogue" at their Web site at:

www.baseballexp.com

FOOTBALL AMERICA

If you coach or play football or if you like to wear football jerseys, this catalog is perfect for you. Football America is your onestop-shop to get all the equipment and football supplies you'll ever need. For your free catalog, call toll-free 877- 697- 7678. Or 109 on at. www.footballamerica.com

Cars & Drivers

A SAFER CAR

Injury, Collision and Theft Losses and *Shopping For A Safer Car* are two guides that will help you make an intelligent choice of the safest vehicle for you. They provide you with excellent safety and loss comparisons for hundreds of passenger cars, vans, pick ups and utility vehicle models. Write to:
INSURANCE INSTITUTE FOR HIGHWAY SAFETY
1005 N. GLEBE RD., SUITE 800
ARLINGTON, VA 22201

IS A TUNE-UP REALLY NEEDED?

Whether you have a new car or an older one, you want to be prepared for any trouble you may encounter. Most of us are trusting souls when it comes to car repair. We rely on the mechanic as the expert. When he tells us the car needs a tune-up, we do it immediately. The Car Council wants us to be aware of *The Eight Most Common Signs Your Car Needs a Tune-Up*. In this booklet you'll find easy to understand advice you can use. It's yours free from:
THE CAR COUNCIL   DEPT T
42 PARK DRIVE
PORT CLINTON OH 43452
WWW.CARCARECOUNCIL.ORG

TIRES

Did you know that when you keep your tires properly inflated that the air provides a cushion of protection when you hit a pothole. If the tire is under inflated you could damage the wheel. If it is over inlated the tire will be damaged. For the best information around for caring and protecting your tires send for a free copy of *The Motorist Tire Care and Safety Guide.* Send a SASE to:
RMA
PO BOX 3147
MEDINA, OHIO, 44258
1-800-325-5095 EXT 242
WWW.RMA.ORG

CAR TROUBLE?

Call the National Highway Safety Auto Complaint line for any technical problems you are having with your vehicle that you feel might be the result of a manufacturing defect.
1-888-327-4236
Also: Auto Safety Hotline:
1-800-424-9393

BUY A CAR?
LEASE A CAR?

If you can't decide whether to buy or lease a vehicle you need to have this guide *"A Consumer Education Guide to Leasing vs. Buying"*. It's free from the Federal Reserve Board. Call:
1-202-452-3244
www.federalreserve.gov

"BE A GOOD NEIGHBOR, BE A DESIGNATED DRIVER"

State Farm wants to help give you, your college, civic group or professional organization free designated driver items. They're a colorful way to remind your friends and associates of the importance of safe driving. They will send your group a free designated driver kit. It has a presentation guide, video and sample speeches. Write to:
STATE FARM INSURANCE COMPANIES
DESIGNATED DRIVER PROGRAM
ONE STATE FARM PLAZA
BLOOMINGTON, IL 61710
WWW.STATEFARM.COM

FOR AAA MEMBERS

If you're a member of AAA they offer an excellent tour service. Tell them where you want to drive and they'll give you detailed road maps with your route outlined in pencil. Contact your local AAA office for this service. For more information, you can call AAA at:
1-888-859-5161
WWW.AAAMIDATLANTIC.COM

HELP FOR CAR OWNERS

If you're having problems with your car and can't seem to get satisfaction from the manufacturer don't despair - help is on the way. The National Highway Traffic Safety Commission is anxious to hear about your complaint so they can get to work on it. They've even set up a toll-free hotline for you to call to report your problem. To report your problem, call toll-free:

1-800-424-9393. OR DROP A LINE TO:
THE NATIONAL HIGHWAY SAFETY ADMINISTRATION
400 7TH ST., S.W.
WASHINGTON, DC 20590
www.nhtsa.dot.gov

AUTOMOBILE HOTLINE NUMBERS

If you plan to buy or lease a car in the near future, be sure you get all the information you need to make an intelligent decision. Call the toll-free hotline phone number of the cars you are interested in. They will send you beautiful color product information booklets

ACURA 1-800-TO-ACURA

BMW 1-800-334-4BMW

BUICK 1-800-4-RIVIERA

CADILLAC 1-800-333-4CAD

CHEVY MONTE CARLO & GEO 1-800-950-2438

CHEVY TAHOE (SPANISH) 1-800-950-TAHOE

CHRYSLER 1-800-4-A-CHRYSLER

DODGE 1-800-4-A-DODGE

FORD 1-800-392-3673

GMC SIERRA 1-800-GMC-TRUCK

HONDA .... 1-800-33-HONDA EXT 435

HYUNDAI 1-800-826-CARS

INFINITI 1-800-826-6500

ISUZU 1-800-726-2700

JAGUAR 1-800-4-JAGUAR

JEEP 1-800-925-JEEP

LAND ROVER 1-800-FINE-4WD

LEXUS 1-800-USA-LEXUS

LINCOLN 1-800-392-3673

MERCEDES 1-800-FOR-MERCEDES

MITSUBISHI 1-800-55-MITSU

NISSAN 1-800-NISSAN-3

OLDMOBILE 1-800-442-6537

PONTIAC 1-800-2-PONTIAC

PORSCHE 1-800-PORSCHE

SAAB .... 1-800-582-SAAB EXT 201

SUBARU 1-800-WANT-AWD

SUZUKI 1-877-697-5985

TOYOTA 1-800-GO-TOYOTA

VOLKSWAGEN 1-800-DRIVE-VW

VOLVO 1-800-550-5658

Travel

TRAVELODGE DIRECTORY

There's a *free directory* of the more than 500 TraveLodge motels and motor hotels waiting for you. It lists location, room rates and a map for each TraveLodge. You'll also find information on their new group rates, family plan and bargain break weekends. Call: TraveLodge International at:
1-800-578-7878
Or visit them on the web: www.travelodge.com

JET VACATIONS

Want to save money on quality air travel, hotels, car rental, ski packages, sightseeing, everything. Paris, France and the Riviera are their speciality. Plan your trip early. Call toll-free and learn how you can enjoy France 3,435 different ways. Call:
1-877-7-TRAVEL

BEFORE YOU TRAVEL

Planning a trip? Before you go you'll want to get a copy of *Lightening The Travel Load Travel Tips*. This handy booklet is filled with "how-to" materials on selecting, packing, traveling and caring for luggage. Send a card to:
SAMSONITE CONSUMER RELATIONS
PO Box 90124
ALLENTOWN, **PA 18109**
WWW. SAMSONITE.COM

IMPORTING A CAR

Can you save money by buying a foreign car on your next trip abroad? What are the customs requirements? What should you know about emission standards on a car you import yourself? For answers, drop a card asking for *Importing A Car* and *U.S. Customs Pocket Hints*. Free from:
U.S. CUSTOMS SERVICE

1300 PENNYSLVANIA AVE
WASHINGTON, DC 20229
WWW.CUSTOMS.GOV

CLUB MED VACATION

Club Med's unique vacation resorts have delighted thousands of people tired of 'the same old thing'. If you're interested in a fun vacation that really is something different, send for the free color *travel booklet* from Club Med by calling:
1-800-CLUB-MED
Or visit them on the web at: www.clubmed.com

DAYS INNS

Quality accommodations for the American traveler at economical rates has been the motto of Days Inn since its founding in 1970. For a *free directory* of the more than 300 Days Inns and 229 Tasty World Restaurants with their rates, maps, toll free numbers and more, call: **1-800-325-2525**
www.daysinn.com

"HOLIDAY INN DIRECTORY"

For a complete listing of Holiday Inns in the U.S. and worldwide, request a free copy of their huge directory. In seconds you can locate any of the thousands of Holiday Inns with room rates, list of recreation activities, even a map for each hotel. Call toll free:
1-800-HOLIDAY.
WWW.SIXCONTINENTHOTELS.COM/HOLIDAY-INN

BAREFOOT CRUISE

Ready for something different? For a vacation unlike any you've ever been on, consider sailing a tall ship to a small island in the Caribbean. The full color *"Barefoot Adventure"* will tell you all about 'Barefoot' shipboard adventures aboard schooners that once belonged to Onassis, Vanderbilt and the Duke of Westminster. Call toll free:
1-800-327-2600.
Or visit their web site at:
www.windjammer.com

Traveling The USA

Planning ahead can make the all important difference between having tons of fun and having a boring vacation.

One important source of information is the tourist offices for the states you plan to visit. These offices are set up to provide maps, brochures and other information about the tourist attractions, climate, restaurants and hotels for their states.

When you write to them, specify which areas of the state you plan to visit and indicate any special sight-seeing interests you may have. Often they can provide you with additional materials on the areas that interest you most.

If you plan to tour any part of the U.S.A. write to the tourist offices of each of the 50 states you intend to visit. Be sure to write well in advance of your trip (a postcard will do). The following is a selected list of state tourism offices. If a toll-free 800 number or a web site is available, it is given.

ALABAMA
Bureau of Tourism & Travel
P.O. Box 4927
Montgomery, AL 36103
1-800-ALABAMA
www.touralabama.org

ALASKA
Alaska Division of Tourism
P.O. Box 110801
Juneau, AK 99811-0801
907-929-2200
www.travelalaska.com

ARIZONA
Arizona Office of Tourism
2702 N. 3rd Street
Suite 4015
Phoenix, AZ 85004
602-230-7733
www.arizonaguide.com
www.azot.com

ARKANSAS
Arkansas Department of Parks and Tourism
1 Capitol Mall
Little Rock, AR 72201
1-800-NATURAL
www.arkansas.com

CALIFORNIA
California Office of Tourism
Department of Commerce
PO Box 1499 Dept TIA
Sacramento, CA 95812
800-862-2543
www.gocalif.ca.gov

COLORADO
Colorado Tourism Board
P.O. Box 3524
Englewood, CO 80150
800-433-2656
Ask for a vacation planning kit
www.colorado.com

CONNECTICUT
Tourism Promotion Service
CT Dept. of Economic
Development
865 Brook Street
Rocky Hill, CT 06067
800-CT-BOUND (nationwide)
www.ctbound.org

DELAWARE
Delaware Tourism Office
Delaware Development Office
99 Kings Highway
PO. Box 1401
Dover, DE 19903
1-800-441-8846 (both in & out
of state)
www.delaware.gov

DISTRICT OF COLUMBIA
Washington Convention and
Visitors Association
1212 New York Ave., NW 600
Washington, DC 20005
1-800-635-6338
   www.washington.org

FLORIDA
Department of Commerce
Visitors Inquiry
126 Van Buren St
Tallahassee, FL 32399
1-888-735-2872
www.flausa.com

GEORGIA
Tourist Division
P.O. Box 1776
Atlanta, GA 30301-1776
1-800 VISIT GA
(1 800 847-4842)
www.georgia.org

HAWAII
Hawaii Visitors Bureau
2270 Kalakaua Ave. Suite 801
Honolulu, HI 96815
1-800-464-2924
www.gohawaii.com

IDAHO
Department of Commerce
700 W. State St. 2nd Fl.
Boise, ID 83720
1-800-635-7820
www.accessidaho.org

ILLINOIS
Illinois Department of
Commerce and Commu-
nity Affairs Tourist Information
100 W. Randolph St.
Ste 3-400
Chicago, IL 60601
1-800-2-CONNECT
www.enjoyillinois.com

INDIANA
Indiana Dept. of
Commerce
Tourism & Film
Development Division
One North Capitol Suite
700
Indianapolis, IN 46204-
2288
1-800-ENJOYIN
www.enjoyindiana.com

IOWA
Iowa Department of
Economic Development
Division of Tourism
200 East Grand Avenue
Des Moines, IA 50309
1-800-472-6035
www.traveliowa.com

KANSAS
Travel & Tourism
Development Division
Department of Commerce
700 SW Harrison
Topeka, KS 66603-3712
1-800-2-KANSAS
www.kansascommerce.com

KENTUCKY
Department of Travel
Development Dept. MR
PO. Box 2011
Frankfort, KY 40602
1-800-225-TRIP
www.kentuckytourism.com

LOUISIANA
Office of Tourism
PO. Box 94291
Baton Rouge, LA 70804
1-800-964-7321
www.louisanatravel.com

MAINE
Maine Publicity Bureau
P.O. Box 2300
Hallowell, ME 04347
1-888-624-6345
www.visitmaine.com

MARYLAND
Office of Tourism Development
217 E. Redwood St.
Baltimore, MD 21202
1-800-MD-IS-FUN
www.mdisfun.org

MASSACHUSETTS
Executive Office of Economic
Affairs
Office of Travel and Tourism
100 Cambridge St., 13th Fl
Boston, MA 02202
1-800-447-MASS
www.massvacation.com

MICHIGAN
Travel Bureau
Department of Commerce
P.O. Box 30226
Lansing, MI 48909
1-800-5432-YES
www.michigan.org

MINNESOTA
Minnesota Office of Tourism
121 7th Place East Suite 100
Metro-Square Bldg.
St. Paul, MN 55101
1-800-657-3700
www.exploreminnesota.com

MISSISSIPPI
Mississippi Division of Tourism
P.O. Box 1705
Ocean Springs, MS 39566
1-800-927-6378
www.visitmississippi.org

MISSOURI
Missouri Division of Tourism
Truman State Office Bldg.
301 W. High St.
PO. Box 1055
Jefferson City, MO 65102
1-800-877-1234
www.missourtourism.org

MONTANA
Department of Commerce
Travel Montana
1424 9th Avenue
Helena, MT 59620
1-800-VISIT-MT
www.visitmt.com

NEBRASKA
Dept of Economic
Development
Division of Travel and Tourism
301 Centennial Mall S.
P.O. Box 94666
Lincoln, NE 68509
1-800-228-4307
www.visitnebraska.org

NEVADA
Commission on Tourism
Capitol Complex
Carson City, NV 89710
1-800-NEVADA-8
www.travelnevada.com

NEW HAMPSHIRE
Office of Vacation Travel
P.O. Box 856
Concord, NH 03302
1-800-FUN-IN-NH
 or for recorded weekly
events, ski conditions, foliage
reports 1-800-258-3608
www.visitnh.gov

NEW JERSEY
Division of Travel and Tourism
20 West State Street
Trenton, NJ 08625
1-800-JERSEY-7 or 1-800-VISITNJ
www.visitnj.org

NEW MEXICO
New Mexico Dept of Tourism
Lamy Bldg.
491 Old Santa Fe Trail
Santa Fe, NM 87503
1-800 545-2040 or 1-800-733-6396
www. newmexico.org

NEW YORK
NYS Tourism
Box 992,
Latham, NY 12110
or call 1-800-CALL NYS
www.iloveny.state.ny.us

NORTH CAROLINA
Travel and Tourism Division
Department of Economic &
Community Development
430 North Salisbury St.
Raleigh, NC 27611
1-800-VISIT-NC
www.visitnc.com

NORTH DAKOTA
North Dakota Tourism
Promotion
Liberty Memorial Building
Capitol Grounds
604 E. Boulevard
Bismarck, ND 58505
1-800-435-5663
www.ndtourism.com

OHIO
Ohio Division of Travel and
Tourism
Vern Riffe Center
77 S. High Street
Columbus, OH 43215
1-800-BUCKEYE
www.ohiotourism.com

OKLAHOMA
Oklahoma Tourism and
Recreation Dept.
Literature Distribution
Center
2401 N. Lincoln Suite 500
Oklahoma City, OK 73105
1-800-652-6552
www.travelok.com

OREGON
Tourism Division
Oregon Economic
Development Dept.
775 Summer St. NE
Salem, OR 97310
1-800-547-7842
www.traveloregon.com

PENNSYLVANIA
Bureau of Travel Marketing
453 Forum Building
Harrisburg, PA 17120
1-800-VISIT PA, ext. 257
www.experiencepa.com

RHODE ISLAND
Rhode Island Tourism
Division
One West Exchange St.
Providence, RI 02903
1-800-556-2484
www.travelsc.com

SOUTH CAROLINA
South Carolina Division of
Tourism
Parks and Recreation
P.O. Box 71
Columbia, SC 29202
1-800-872-3505
www.travelsc.com

SOUTH DAKOTA
Department of Tourism
711 E. Wells Ave.
Pierre, South Dakota 57501
1-800-SDAKOTA
www.travelsd.com

TENNESSEE
Department of Tourist
Development
P.O. Box 23170
Nashville, TN 37202
1-800-836-6200
www.state.tn.us/tourdev

TEXAS
Travel Information Services
Texas Department of
Transportation
P.O. Box 5064
Austin, TX 78763 5064
1-800-8888-TEX or 800-452-9292
www.travelTEX.com

UTAH
Utah Travel Council
Council Hall, Capitol Hill
Salt Lake City, UT 84114
1-800-200-1160
www.utah.com

VERMONT
Agency of Development and
Community Affairs
Travel Division
134 State St.
Montpelier, VT 05602
1-800-VERMONT
www.1-800-vermont.com

VIRGINIA
Virginia Department of Economic
Development
Tourism Development Group
River Front Plaza W. 19th Fl.
Richmond, VA 23219
1-800-VISIT-VA
www.virginia.org

WASHINGTON
Washington State Dept. of Trade
and Economic Development
101 General Administration Bldg.
P.O. Box 42500
Olympia, WA 98504
1-800-544-1800
www.experiencewashington.com

WASHINGTON, D.C.
See District of Columbia

WEST VIRGINIA
Division of Tourism and Parks
State Capitol Complex
Bldg. #6 Room #564
1900 Kanawha Blvd. East
Charleston, WV 25305-0317
1-800 CALL-WVA
www.callwva.com

WISCONSIN
Travel Information
Division of Tourism
123 W. Washington Ave.
P.O. Box 7606
Madison, WI 53707
1-800-432-TRIP
www.travelwisconsin.com

WYOMING
Wyoming Division of Tourism
I-25 at College Drive
Cheyenne, WY 82002
1-800-225-5996
www.wyomingtourism.org

US TERRITORIES
American Samoa
1-684-633-1093
www.amsamoa.com

GUAM
1-800-US-3-GUAM
www.visitguam.org

PUERTO RICO
1-800-223-6530
www.prtourism.com

US VIRGIN ISLANDS
US Virgin Islands Tourism
1270 Ave. of the Americas,
Ste. 2108
New York, NY 10020
1-800-372-8784
www.usvi.net

NATIONAL PARKS

Enjoy the great outdoors. Get back to nature. Visit our beautiful national parks. There's a series of interesting guides to the 7 most popular national parks free for the asking. Send for any (or all) guides you'd like:

"Rocky Mountain National Park, Colorado"
"Mt. McKinley National Park, Alaska"
"Mesa Verde National Park Colorado"
'Hot Springs National Park, Arkansas"
"Hawaii National Park"
"Yellowstone National Park"
"Carlsbad Caverns, New Mexico"..

You might also want the *free map* of the National Park System. Request by name the guides you would like. Write to:

DEPT. OF THE INTERIOR
NATIONAL PARK SERVICE
WASHINGTON, DC 20240

CHOCOLATE TOWN USA

If you are looking for a really fun time, why not try a special theme weekend at the fun Hershey Park in Hershey, Pennsylvania. For more detailed information, call:

1-800-HERSHEY
WWW.HERSHEYPA.COM

INTERNATIONAL VACATIONLAND— 1000 ISLANDS

The 1000 Islands region features the best of two countries — U.S. and Canada. Some of the many attractions include fishing, golf, tennis, biking, hiking, houseboat rentals, shopping and recreational sports in all seasons. Three tour packages are available for the asking:

1. Write: **1000 Islands, 43373 Collins Landing, PO Box 400 Alexandria Bay, NY 13607.** (In Canada write: 1000 Islands, Box 69, Landsdoune, Ontario KOE ILO Or call: **1-800-8-ISLAND**

2. Write: **Kingston Bureau of Tourism, Box 486, 209 Ontario St., Kingston, Ontario K7L 2ZI Or call: 1-888-855-4555**

3. Write: **Rideau Lakes Thousand Islands, P.O. Box 125 Perth, Ontario K7H 3E3**

NEED DIRECTIONS?

Planning a trip, or visiting long lost friends but aren't sure how to get there. If you have a computer all you have to do type in where you are and where you are going and Map Quest.com will plot out your trip for you. You can also print out a map with clear and concise directions to follow. Log on to their website at:
www.mapquest.com

Foreign Travel

ANGUILLA
Anguilla Tourist Information
271 Main Street
Northport, NY 11768

ANTIGUA & BARBUDA
Antigua & Barbuda Dept of Tourism
610 Fifth Avenue, Suite 311
New York, NY 10020
1-888-268-4227
www.antigua-barbuda.org

ARGENTINA
For maps and color brochures describing Argentina drop a
card to:
Argentina Embassy
1600 New Hampshire Ave.
Washington, DC 20009
1-202-238-6400
www.embajadaargentina-usa.org

ARUBA
Go sailing, scuba diving in the turquoise Caribbean,
casinos, discos and lots more. Ask for "Sun Worshippers"
with hotel rates and tourist information. Write:
Aruba Tourist Office
1000 Harbor Boulevard
Weehawken, NJ 07087
1-800-TO-ARUBA
www.aruba.com

AUSTRIA
Write for the *"Austrian Information package"* and you'll
receive a beautiful assortment of travel guides and student
education opportunities. Drop a card to: Austrian National
Tourist Office
PO BOX 1142
New York, NY 10180-1142
1-212-6880, fax: 1-212-730-4568
www.austria-tourism.at

BAHAMAS
Bahamas Tourist Office
1-800-422-4262
www.bahamas.com

BARBADOS

Discover the many sides of Barbados that make it a luscious vacation spot. A nice tow *package* including several huge wall posters are yours for the asking. Write:
Barbados Board of Tourism
800 Second Ave.
New York, NY 10017
1-800-221-9831
www.barbados.org

BELIZE

Belize Tourist Board
New Central Bank Bldg. Level 2
Gabourel Lane
PO Box 325
Belize City, Belize
Central America
1-800-624-0686
www.travelbelize.org

BRAZIL

Brazil Reservations
1050 Edison St., Ste. C
Santa Ynez, CA 93460
1-800-544-5503
www.brazilres.com

BRITISH VIRGIN ISLANDS

British Tourist Board
370 Lexington Avenue Ste. 1605
New York, NY 10017
1-212-696-0400
www.bviwelcome.com

BRITAIN

There's always something new to discover in England, Wales, Scotland & Ireland. Drop a card requesting the *Britain Information package* and you'll receive a beautiful color magazine, photos, maps, tours, etc. Send to:
British Tourist Authority
551 Fifth Ave.
New York, NY. 10176
1-800-462-2748
www.visitbritain.com

BRITAIN BY RAIL

Tour scenic Britain by rail. BritRail offers unlimited travel on most rail, bus & ferry routes. For a free guide travel hints as well as bargain ticket rates write to:
Europerail International
691 Richmond St.

London, Ontario, Canada N6A 5MI
1-888-667-9734
www.britainontrack.com

BERMUDA

Thinking of traveling to Bermuda? Don't go without this
information *package*. It includes travel tips, a map, hotel
rates, and more. Write to:
Bermuda Dept. of Tourism.
205 E. 42 St. 16th flr.
New York, NY 11377
1-800-237-6832 for brochures
1-800-223-6106 Dept. of Tourism
www.bermudatourism.org

CANADA

"Touring Canada" is a big guide to 54 exciting tours of Canada.
You'll learn where to go, what to see, what clothes to bring
and much more. You'll find there's more to do in 'our neighbor to the north' than you had ever imagined. Write to:
Canadian Tourism Commission
235 Queen St., 8th flr. West
Ottawa, Ontario
Canada K1A OH6
1-613-1000
www.canadatourism.com

CANADA-NOVA SCOTIA

Nova Scotia Information
2695 Dutch Village Rd., Ste, 501
Halifax, Nova Scotia
Canada B3L 4V2
1-800-341-6096
www.checkinnovascotia.com

CANCUN & COZUMEL

Caribbean Tourism Organization
 80 Broad St., 32nd flr.
New York, NY 10004
1-212-635-9530
www.doitcaribbean.com

CARIBBEAN SUN FUN

Discover the fun and excitement each of the Caribbean islands has to offer. Ask for the *travel package*
free from:
Caribbean Tourism Organization
80 Broad St., 32nd flr.
New York, NY 10004
1-212-635-9530
www.doitcaribbean.com

CAYMAN ISLANDS
Cayman Islands Tourism
420 Lexington Avenue, Ste. 2733
New York, NY 10170
1-212-682-5582
www.cayman.org/tourism

CHINA - TAIWAN
Taiwan Visitors Association
One World Trade Center
New York, NY

CURACAO
Curacao Tourist Board
475 Park Ave. South Suite 2000
New York, NY 10016
1-800-445-8266
1-800-328-7222
www.curacao-tourism.com

EGYPT
Travel back in time to the cradle of civilization. Explore the
pyramids and discover the old and new wonders of Egypt.
Ask for the *Egypt Information package.* Write to: Egyptian
Tourist Authority
630 Fifth Ave. Ste. 1706
New York, NY 10111
1-212-332-2570
www.egypttourism.org

FRANCE
The *France Information package* is a mini-tour of France
with a large full color tour book plus Paris on a budget, a
tour of Paris, hotels and motels in France off-season
packages, and more. Contact:
French Government Tourist Office
444 Madison Ave. 16th flr.
New York, NY 10022
1-212-838-7800
www.francetourism.com

GERMANY
"Welcome To Germany" is a beautiful guide full of color
photos that are absolutely breathtaking. This is just part of
the Germany Tour package free from:
German National Tourist Office
122 E. 42 St., 52nd flr.
New York, NY 10168-7200
1-212-661-7200
www.visit-to-germany.com

GERMANY TRAIN TRAVEL
If you're planning a trip to Germany one of the best ways to tour the country is by train. With German Rail you will have unlimited travel plus discounts on many bus and boat routes. For free information write:
DER Travel Services
9501 W. Devon Ave., Ste. 1E
Rosemont, IL 60018
1-888-337-7350
www.dertravel.com
1-800-660-5300
www.eurorail.com/germrail.htm

BERLIN
This city is the Gateway to Continental Europe. You can experience the mix of Berlin's dynamic culture, historic sights and non- stop nightlife. Call for your free *Berlin Travel kit* today. Call 1-800-248-9539

GREECE
To help you make your trip to Greece more enjoyable, here's a large packet of bro- chures, maps and booklets on the beautiful Greek Islands. Request the *Greece Tour package* from:
Greek National Tourist Organization
645 Fifth Ave., 9th flr. Olympic Tower
New York, NY 10022
1-212-421-5777
www.gnto.gr

GRENADA
Grenada Board of Tourism
800 Second Avenue, Suite 400K
New York, NY 10017
1-800-927-9554
www.grenada.org

GUYANA
Guyana Tourism
c/o Caribbean Tourism Organization
80 Broad Street 32nd flr.
New York, NY 10004
1-212-635-9630
www.doitcaribbean.com

HONG KONG
Hong Kong Tourism Board
115 E. 54 St., 2nd flr.
New York, NY 10022
1-800-282-4582
www.discoverhongkong.com/usa

HUNGARY
Like beautiful picture post cards, the color illustrations in this package will take you for a tour of the sights and attractions of Hungary. Ask for the *Hungary Travel package* which includes a map of the country. Send a card to:
Hungary National Tourist Board
150 E. 58th St. 33rd flr.
New York, NY 10155
1-212-355-0240
www.go2hungary.com

INDIA
Dozens of scenic color photos of India are included in the *India Tour Kit* yours free from:
Information Service of India
Embassy of India
2107 Massachusetts Ave. NW
Washington, DC 20008
1-202-939-7000
www.indiamart.com

INDONESIA
For facts on the Indonesia archipelago including their history, geography, culture, maps, and more drop a card requesting their *information package.* Write to: Consulate General of Indonesia
Information Section
Five E. 68th St.
New York, NY 10021
1-212-879-0600
www.indony.org

IRELAND
Irish Tourist Board
345 Park Ave., 17th flr.
New York, NY 10154
1-800-SHAMROCK
1-800-223-6470
www.ireland.travel.ie

ISRAEL
If you enjoyed the book you'll love the country. For a nice collection of *guide books and maps* of Israel and the Holy Land write to:
Israel Government Tourist Office
800 Second Ave., 16 flr.
New York, NY 10117
1-888-77-ISRAEL
www.goisrael.com

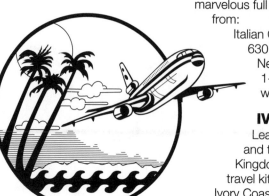

ITALY

A beautiful arm chair tour of Italy is in store for you. Write for *"A Trip To Italy tour package"* with road maps and marvelous full color guide books. It's yours free from:

Italian Government Travel Office
630 Fifth Ave., Ste. 1565
New York, NY 10111
1-212-245-4822/5618
www.italiantourism.com

IVORY COAST

Learn about the rites of Panther Men and the fascinating culture of the Agri Kingdom. All this and much more in the travel kit from:
Ivory Coast Embassy
3421 Massachusetts Ave. NW
Washington, DC 20007
1-202-797-0337
www.embassy.org/embassies/ci.html

JAMAICA

Soft beaches, jungle waterfalls, hot discos and sailing in the sunshine—it's all in a beautiful full color book that features 56 great vacations. Ask for the free *"Jamaica Vacation Book"* from:
Jamaica Tourist Board
1320 S. Dixie Hwy., Ste. 1101
Coral Gables, FL 33146
www.jamaicatravel.com

JAPAN

The *Japan Tour package is* an impressive collection of travel booklets in full color with marvelous illustrations. You'll receive a mini tour of Japan chuck full of facts about Japan's history with travel tips and many fascinating tid bits. For all this write to:
Japan Travel Bureau
810 Seventh Ave., 34th flr.
New York NY 10019
1-212-698-4900
www.jtbusa.com

MARTINIQUE

Martinique Promotion Bureau
444 Madison Ave., 16th flr.
New York, NY 10022
1-800-391-4909
www.martinique.org

MEXICO
For a set of over a dozen color brochures showing the
sights and tourist attractions of Mexico, drop a post card
to:
The Magic of Mexico
1-800-44-MEXICO
www.visitmexico.com

MONTSERRAT
Caribbean Tourism Organization
80 Broad St., 32nd flr.
New York, NY 10004
1-212-635-9530
www.doitcaribbean.com

MOROCCO
Exotic Morocco has some of the most magnificent scenery
in the world. For a kit of *travel information and tour packages* to this ancient kingdom drop a card to:
Royal Air Maroc
55 East 59th St.
New York, NY 10022
1-212-750-6071
www.royalairmaroc.com

PERU
In this package are colorful maps, charts and pictures of
native birds, flowers and animals. You'll also find a listing of
national parks and reserves, as well as interesting archaeo-
logical and historical highlights.
Explorations, Inc.
27655 Kent Rd.
Bonita Springs, Fl 34135
1-941-992-9660
member.aol.com/xplormaya

PORTUGAL
Discover all the beauty of Portugal— its beaches, entertainment and hotels — all in this package of full color brochures.
Portugese National Touris Office
590 Fifth Ave., 4th flr.
New York, NY 10036
1-212-220-5772
www.portugalinsite.pt

PUERTO RICO
Find out why Puerto rico is called "the complete
island". There is something here for everyone —
sightseeing, sports, night life, casinos and lots more.
Call: 1-212-599-6262

RUSSIA
Embassy of the Russian Federation
2650 Wisconsin Ave. NW
Washington, DC 20007
1-202-298-5700
www.russiaembassy.org

ST. MAARTEN
For beautiful travel brochures of the island of St. Maarten
call: 1-800-ST-MAARTEN
WWW.TRAVELFACTS.COM/FACTS/HTM/SXM/SXMDEST/
HTM

SCOTLAND
For colorful brochures on Scotland, call toll-free:
1-800-343-SCOT
www.toscotland.com

SINGAPORE
Singapore's the place where all Asia comes together.
Here's a beautiful color package of things to do and
see plus a map and even a recipe booklet with delightful meals of Singapore. Write to:
Embassy of Republic of Singapore
3501 International Pl. NW
Washington, D.C. 20008
1-202-537-3100

SOUTH AFRICA
Write to:
Embassy of South Africa
3501 Massachusetts Ave. N.W.
Washington, D.C. 20008
1-202-232-4400
http://usaembassy.southafrica.net

SPAIN
Write to:
Tourist Office of Spain
666 Fifth Ave., 35th flr.
New York, NY 10103
1-212-265-8822

SWITZERLAND
For a mini-tour of the Alps send a postcard for the
Swiss Tour package. You'll receive beautifully illus-
trated booklets, maps, travel tips, recipes and more.
All of this comes to you free from:

Swiss National Tourist Office
608 Fifth Ave., Ste. 202
New York, NY 10020
1-212-757-5944
www.myswitzerland.com

TAIWAN
Taiwan Visitors Association
405 Lexington Ave., 37th flr.
New York, NY 10174
1-212-867-1632
www.tbroc.gov.tw

THAILAND
Come to Thailand and enjoy its dazzling scenery,
incredible shopping bargains and the special joy of
sharing all they have. Drop a card to:
Tourism Authority of Thailand
611 N. Larchmont Blvd., 1st flr.
 Los Angeles, CA 90004
1-800-Thailand
www.tourismthailand.org

ZAMBIAN SAFARI
Zambia has a big package of travel & tourist information waiting for you. The beautiful color brochures are
a mini-safari through the African bush. Write to:
Zambia National Tourist Board
237 E. 52nd St.
New York, NY 10022
1-202-265-9717

Money Matters

FREE HELP PLANNING FOR YOUR FUTURE

If you were going on a trip, you would never just hop in your car and start driving. Before you left you would have a clear set of directions in hand so you could get to where you were going without problems. Nevertheless, it's amazing how many people forge ahead with absolutely no planning for their future, no clear destination in mind and no plan on how to get there.

If that sounds like something you would like to avoid, here are a variety of booklets that will help you plan ahead:

Planning Today for a Secure Tomorrow - Describes the financial planning process and how it will help you define and reach your life goals.

Seeking Professional Advice - Provides information on the role financial advisors play in the financial planning process and how advisors can offer knowledge and guidance to help you reach your life goals.

Selecting Your Financial Advisor - Outlines steps to take in learning about a financial adviser, finding one that will best fit your needs and building trust with that adviser.

Providing For An Enriching Retirement - Guides you through key issues to consider in providing for retirement, including setting goals and making lifestyle decisions.

Leaving A Legacy - Discusses estate planning, charitable giving and ways to provide for loved ones after you are gone.

Understanding Your Assets and Invest-ments - Demystifies assets and invest-ments, defines terms such as volatility and diversification, and shows how to make smart decisions with the help of an adviser.

Funding Higher Education - Discusses el-ements to consider when funding education such as loans and long-term savings and describes the role financial planning pays in preparing for higher education costs.

Preparing For Long-Term Health Care - Outlines decisions surrounding long-term care and health in later years, including in-surance and security needs.

Managing Your Taxes - Provides ideas on mini-mizing taxes, planning for coming years, using de-ductions effectively and handling an audit.

All of these publications are yours free from The International Association For Financial Planning. Visitors to the web site or callers to the toll-free number can also ask for a list of financial plan-ners in their area. Call them at:
1-888-806-PLAN
Or you can visit their web site at:
www.planningpaysoff.org.

FINANCIAL ADVISER
Everybody, regardless of age, should have a finan-cial adviser. Just remember it's never to late to build a nest egg. Oppenheimer Funds Inc. has pub-lished a guide *Finding A Financial Adviser Who's Right For You.* This will take you through the pro-cess step by step of selecting names, conducting interviews, making the final decision, and main-taining a relationship that will be profitable. This is a must for anyone looking for help in making intelligent financial planning decisions. To order your free copy call:
1-888-470-0862
www.oppenheimerfunds.com

MONEY FACTS

The federal Reserve Bank of Atlanta has a free booklet that describes how currency is designed, printed, circulated and eventully destroyed. There's even a section on how to redeem damaged bills. Ask for *Fundamental Facts about U.S. Money.* Write to:
FEDERAL RESERVE BANK OF ATLANTA
PUBLIC AFFAIRS DEPT.
ATLANTA, GA. 30303

FAST BANKING

The American Bankers Association's free brochure on *A Dozen Ways to Save Time and Money at the Bank* offers a variety of tips on money management. For a free copy, write to:
ATTENTION: 'A DOZEN TIPS.'
THE AMERICAN BANKERS ASSOCIATION
1120 CONNECTICUT AVE. N.W.
WASHINGTON, D.C. 20036

NEW VENTURE

If you are thinking of going into business and starting a new corporation, here's a booklet you will definitely want to get. *Starting Your Own Corporation* will answer many of the questions you may have regarding setting up the right kind of corporation. For your free copy, call the "Corporation Company" at **1-800-542-2677.**

CHOOSING THE MORTGAGE THAT'S RIGHT FOR YOU

Ready to shop for a mortgage? This easy to read 40 page guide can help. It walks you through the mortgage shopping process in three easy steps. How big a mortgage loan you can afford, choosing a mortgage that's right for you, and comparing terms among lenders. This guide is free from:
FANNIE MAE
PO BOX 27463
RICHMOND, VA 23286-8999
OR CALL 1-800 688-HOME
www.fanniemae.com

TAX DO'S & DON'TS FOR MUTUAL FUND INVESTORS

This 20 page booklet lists 13 points to consider about the tax aspects of mutual fund investing. For example, it warns you *not* to assume that all fund distributions are the same, that you owe no taxes on reinvested dividends or that you owe no tax if you exchange shares from one fund for shares of another in mutual fund 'families.' For a copy of the free booklet write to:
**ICI
1401 H ST. N.W., SUITE 1200
WASHINGTON, D.C. 20005**

HELP WITH YOUR TAXES

When tax time comes around it's always a good idea to have a tax pro help you. For the names of tax experts in your area, call the National Association of Enrolled Agents:
**1-800 424-4339
www.naea.org**

INVESTING FOR RETIREMENT

IRA Transfers is a free brochure that tax-sheltered retirement investing. It can help you get the most from your investments. It is published by the AARP Investment Program from Scudder, Stevens & Clark - a group of no-load mutual funds designed for members of the AARP, but open to investors of any age. (No-load means there is no sales commission.) For a copy, call:
1-800-322-2282, EXT. 8271

The State Tax Laws: A Guide for Investors Aged 50 and Over is another free publication from AARP. Scudder prepared this 112 page guide in conjunction with the National Conference of State Legislatures. For a copy call:
1(800-322-2282, EXT 8254

PERSONAL FINANCE HELPLINES

If you are not sure where to turn for good advice regarding your personal finances, here are several toll-free hotlines you can turn to for help. They will either provide you with the information you need or they will tell you where you can go for further assistance.

FINANCIAL PLANNING

THE INSTITUTE OF CERTIFIED FINANCIAL PLANNERS – FOR BROCHURES & REFERRALS, CALL **1-800-282-7526**
THE AMERICAN INSTITUTE OF CERTIFIED PUBLIC ACCOUNTANTS' PERSONAL FINANCIAL PLANNING DIVISION CALL: **1-888-777-7077**
THE INTERNATIONAL ASSOCIATION FOR FINANCIAL PLANNING CALL: **(404) 395-1605** (NOT TOLL-FREE)
THE NATIONAL ASSOCIATION OF PERSONAL FINANCIAL ADVISERS CALL: **1-800 366-2732**
THE AMERICAN SOCIETY OF CLU AND CHFC CALL: **1-800-392-6900**

INVESTMENTS

To find a stockbroker, ask for referrals from friends, relatives, professional acquaintenances. To check a broker's background, call:
THE NATIONAL ASSOCIATION OF SECURITIES DEALERS: **1-800-289-9999**
WWW.NASD.COM

SOCIAL SECURITY

For an estimate of what your retirement benefits might be call: **1-800-772-1213** and ask for an *'earnings estimate request'* to fill out and return.

CURRENCY SAVERS

Did your dog chew up some money you left on the table? Well the U.S. Department of Treasury can help restore that money for you. Drop them a line with a plausible detailed explanation. Once the claim is processsed the actual payment is made by federal check. For more information write:
U.S. DEPARTMENT OF THE TREASURY
OFFICE OF CURRENCY STANDARDS
15TH STREET & PENNSYLVANIA AVE., N.W.
WASHINGTON, D.C. 20220
OR CALL **(1-202) 622-2000**

MORTGAGES

If you are looking for a new mortgage but are not

sure what you should do to get the mortgage that is best for you, there's a toll-free number to First Financial Equity you can call for more information and for answers to your all your questions. Call them toll-free:
1-800-454-0505

INVESTMENTS

Before you make any significant investment, learn what to look for to find the one that's best for you. Also discover how to evaluate your investment and determine how well it meets your objectives. Ask for *Evaluating Investment Performance* write to:
NEUBERGER & BERMAN
INDIVIDUAL ASSET MANAGEMENT GROUP
605 THIRD AVE.
NEW YORK, NY 10158
OR CALL: **1-877-672-7329**

OVER 50?

Now that a large portion of the population is over 50 years old, there are lots of bargains and discounts available just for the asking. Remember if you don't ask you'll never know. Always check to see if there are certain days or certain times when seniors are offered discounts or specials. Many hotels offer discounts on their rooms as well as disounts if you eat in their restaurants. You can also apply for a travel club card if you are a member of AARP...The American Association of Retired People. You can contact them at:
1-800-424-3410

MUTUAL FUNDS

Learn all about mutual funds and find out which are the best ones for you. Check out the Strong Equity Performers from Dreyfus call: **1-800-782-6620** Or visit a Dreyfus Financial Center via the Internet:
www.dreyfus.com

UTILITIES FUND

Basic utilities such as water and electricity are always in demand and telecommunications is growing in all countries. That's why the Franklin Utili-

ties Fund could be a growth fund for you. They will manage a portfolio especially designed for you. If this sounds like something you would consider, send today for a free brochure:
FRANKLIN TEMPLETON INVESTMENTS
PO BOX 997152
SACRAMENTO, CA 95899
Or call: **1-800-632-2301**
www.franklintempleton.com

FUND RAISING

If your school or organization needs money, this *free fund-raising kit* will teach you how. This kit will help show your group how to collect member's recipes and publish them into a great cookbook. Write for your free kit to:
FUNDCRAFT
BOX 340
COLLIERVILLE, TN 38027
1-800-853-1363
www.fundcraft.com

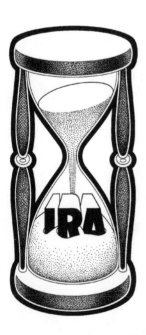

LOW INSURANCE PREMIUMS

If you are in the market for Medicare and Medigap policies for health insurance for yourself or a parent, your premiums will be lowest if you enroll from three months before, to four months after your 65th birthday. After that, the premiums may grow by 10 percent each year you wait. For more information, call **1-800-772-1213** and ask for The Social Security Administration's free *Guide to Health Insurance for People with Medicare* or write:
THE HEALTH INSURANCE ASSOCIATION OF AMERICA
PUBLICATION OFFICE
555 13TH ST. N. W.
SUITE 600-E
WASHINGTON, D.C. 20004

TAX-FREE INCOME FUND

You can start earning tax-free income with as little as $1,000 with prompt liquidity and no sales or redemption fee. Call:
1-800-638-5660
WWW.TROWEPRICE.COM

MUTUAL FUNDS FOR INVESTORS OVER 50

"Understanding Mutual Funds: A Guide for Investors Aged 50"and Over", defines the basics to help older individuals choose funds appropriate for their needs. Absolutely free! Write:
AARP INVESTMENT PROGRAM
811 MAIN STREET
KANSAS CITY< MO 64105
OR CALL: 800-322-2282

MUTUAL FUNDS

To find out more about money market funds, contact one or more of these large funds for their *prospectus and information package:*
DREYFUS SERVICE CORP.
200 PARK AVE.
NEW YORK, NY 10166
1-800-645-6561
WWW.DREYFUS.COM

FIDELITY INVESTMENTS
P.O. BOX 770001
CINCINNATI, OH 45277
CALL 800-544-3902
WWW.FIDELITY.COM

AMERICAN EXPRESS FINANCIAL ADVISORS
70100 AXP FINANCIAL CENTER
MINNEAPOLIS, MN 55474
CALL 1-800-AXP-FUND
finance.americanexpress.com/finance

BE YOUR OWN BROKER

If you have a computer and like to make your own investment decisions without the help of a stockbroker, this one may be for you. Charles Schwab has free computer software you can use to buy and sell securities over the internet for just $29.95 for up to 1,000 shares. The software also allows you to do your own research using various internet databases, track the stocks you are interested in and lots more. For more information call:
1-800-E-SCHWAB
www.schwab.com

IRS OR H & R BLOCK?

Few people realize that the IRS is committed to giving taxpayers every legitimate deduction they're entitled to. The IRS has toll-free numbers throughout the country you can call for assistance and/or forms. The Internal Revenue Service tax hotline for answers to your income tax question is:
1-800-829-1040

The IRS also has a series of helpful publications such as *"Federal Income Tax"* available free of charge. Call the toll-free number for this publication or a list of the others available.

The IRS even has a toll-free number to assist deaf/hearing-impaired taxpayers who have access to TV-Phone/Teletypewriter equipment (800-428-4732; In Indiana — 800-382-4059).

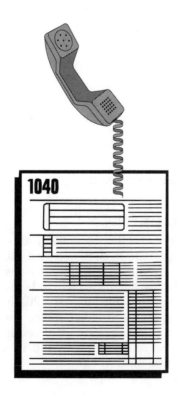

Free From The U.S. Government

PERSONAL EARNINGS & BENEFIT ESTIMATE STATEMENT

This statement tells how much Social Security earnings-year by year- have been reported by your employers, and what your benefits will be if you retire at different ages. Find out what disability benefits you qualify for... and how the value of your benefits compares with the amount of Social Security taxes you have paid. This is free from the Social Security Administration. Call:
1-800-772-1213

MISSING PERSONS

If you have a problem of trying to locate a missing relative or friend, a letter to the Social Security Administration may help. When you write be sure to include as much information as you can about the missing person (including their last address and date of birth). Write to:
PUBLIC INQUIRIES
SOCIAL SECURITY ADMINISTRATION
6501 SECURITY BLVD.
BALTIMORE, MD 20235

STRIKING IT RICH

Did you know that the U.S. Government will let you prospect on public lands? If you would like to find out how to strike it rich on government lands, send a card to the Forest Service. Also ask for *A Guide To Your National Forests*. Write:
MINERALS AND GEOLOGY STAFF
FOREST SERVICE, DOA
BOX 2417
WASHINGTON, DC 20013

BUYING U.S. GOVERNMENT SURPLUS
The U.S. Government must sell surplus property of all types on a regular basis. To find out how to buy everything imagineable from binoculars to furniture and cars at bargain prices, call toll-free:
DEFENSE REUTILIZATION & MARKETING SERVICES
SURPLUS MERCHANDISE -- PUBLIC AFFAIRS DEPT
1-888-352-9333

FREE FIREWOOD
In most of the 154 National Forests firewood for your own personal use, is free. To find out how you can get free firewood and also how to select, purchase and use firewood ask for *Firewood Information*. It's yours free from:
FIREWOOD #559,
FOREST SERVICE
BOX 2417
WASHINGTON, DC 20013

FEDERAL JOB INFORMATION
Various branches of the Federal Government have positions open throughout the U.S. The majority of these jobs are in large metropolitan areas. Drop them a card and ask for *Job Information*. Write:
OFFICE OF PERSONNEL MANAGEMENT
PO BOX 52
WASHINGTON, D.C. 20044

SAVINGS BOND REDEMPTION
Every Series E Savings Bond ever issued (since 1941) is still earning interest. If you own any bonds and would like to know exactly how much they're worth today, write for *Tables of Redemption Values For Savings Bonds* from:
BUREAU OF PUBLIC DEBT
SAVING BOND OPERATIONS
200 THIRD AVE.
PARKERSBURG, WV 26101-1328
Or visit their Web site: www.savingbonds.gov

SECRET SERVICE
The Secret Service does more than protect the President. It was originally created to suppress counter-

feiting - a job they still perform - Ask for *Counterfeiting and Forgery* which shows how to detect a counterfeit bill. Write to:
U.S. SECRET SERVICE
1800 'G' ST. N.W., ROOM 941
WASHINGTON, DC 20223

CRIME RESISTANCE

The F.B.I. would like every family to feel more secure. Learn how to better protect your family against crime. *A Way to Protect Your Family Against Crime* offers tips you and your family can safely use to take a bite out of crime. Ask for the free Crime Resistance booklet. You might also want a copy of *Abridged History of the F.B.I.* All free from:
PUBLIC AFFAIRS DEPT.
F.B.I.
10TH & PENNSYLVANIA AVE.
WASHINGTON, DC 20535

BUYING U.S. GOVERNMENT SECURITIES

Americans have been buying Series E Savings bonds for many years. But few know they can buy Treasury Bonds and Bills that pay even higher interest. For more information on how you can get in on this no-risk, high-yield investment, write for *U.S. Securities Available to Investors*. From:

PUBLIC DEBT INFORMATION
U.S. DEPARTMENT OF THE TREASURY
WASHINGTON, D.C. 20226

Consumer Information From The U.S. Government

Agencies of the U.S. Government publish thousands of documents every year. While many are too technical for general interest, others are of interest to a wide number of consumers. Those that are, are available through:

CONSUMER INFORMATION, PUEBLO CO 81002

Essentially all of the publications listed here are either free or $1.50 or less (for s&h). You can receive up to 25 free publications by simply enclosing $2.00 as a processing fee. (See more complete details at the end of this section.)

HEALTH

COSMETIC LASER SURGERY: A HIGH-TECH WEAPON IN THE FIGHT AGAINST AGING SKIN
Explains how laser surgery can help remove facial wrinkles and lines, how to tell if it's right for you, the risks, and more. 4 pp. 542K. Free.

DRINKING WATER FROM HOUSEHOLD WELLS
Families with their own wells are responsible for maintaining them and checking to see that the water is safe to drink. Here are the facts on sources of pollution and keeping your water safe. 16 pp. 547K. Free.

HOW TO FIND MEDICAL INFORMATION
Use your local library, the federal government, and the Internet to get information on an illness or disorder. 24 pp. 544K. Free.

MAMMOGRAPHY TODAY
How to tell if you are getting a high-quality mammogram, what to do if you need to change mammogram facilities, and more. 6 pp. 511K. Free.

PROTECT YOUR DRINKING WATER
Learn where your water comes from, the factors that affect its quality, and how to prevent pollution. 7 pp. 602K. Free.

STAYING HEALTHY AT 50+
Covers everything from cholesterol levels, various cancers, weight control, and checkups, with helpful charts to keep track of your medications, shots, and screening test results. 64 pp. 141K. $3.00.

YOUR RIGHTS AFTER A MASTECTOMY
Federal law requires health plans to provide certain benefits if you have had a mastectomy. 6 pp. 512K. Free.

DRUGS & HEALTH AIDS

AN ASPIRIN A DAY...JUST ANOTHER CLICHE?
Read about the benefits of taking aspirin to prevent cardiovascular disease and decide if taking it is right for you. 4 pp. 536K. Free.

BUYING PRESCRIPTION MEDICINES ONLINE: A CONSUMER SAFETY GUIDE
Here's a helpful list of do's and don'ts when shopping for medications over the Internet. 5 pp. 526K. Free.

DRUG INTERACTIONS: WHAT YOU SHOULD KNOW
Protect yourself and your family from potentially dangerous interactions of prescription drugs, over-the-counter (OTC) drugs, food, and medical conditions. 8 pp. 527K. Free.

EMERGING TRENDS IN MEDICAL DEVICE TECHNOLOGY: HOME IS WHERE THE HEART MONITOR IS
Learn about the latest home monitoring systems and how they transmit data to your health care provider, the future of these systems, home healthcare issues, and more. 6 pp. 545K. Free.

FDA's TIPS FOR TAKING MEDICINES
Tips to protect yourself from prescription and OTC drugs that may react in strange ways to each other, certain foods, alcohol, etc. 4 pp. 506K. Free.

MY MEDICINES
Take care of yourself with this easy-to-follow guide that features questions to ask your doctor and a

simple chart to keep track of your medications. 6 pp. 528K. Free.

NEW OVER-THE-COUNTER MEDICINE LABEL...
Take a Look! Labels of all OTC medicines are required to have information listed in the same order and presented in a consistent, easier-to-understand manner. See a sample of the new OTC label and what you'll find on it. 5 pp. 557K. Free.

OVER-THE-COUNTER MEDICINES: WHAT'S RIGHT FOR YOU?
Use labeling information to avoid harmful interactions, protect against unsafe products, and get the most effective relief from your symptoms. 12 pp. 520K. Free.

THINK IT THROUGH: A GUIDE TO MANAGING THE BENEFITS AND RISKS OF MEDICINES
Before you start any new medication, protect yourself by asking your doctor the right questions, reading your medications' labels, avoiding harmful interactions, keeping track of the medications you take, and more. 4 pp. 598K. Free.

VISION CORRECTION: TAKING A LOOK AT WHAT'S NEW
Use this guide to learn about the latest developments in laser and non-laser eye surgery, contact lenses, and eyeglasses. 7 pp. 546K. Free.

YOU KNOW THE QUESTIONS THAT GO THROUGH YOUR MIND WHEN YOU TAKE YOUR GENERIC DRUG?
Find out what generic drugs are, how they differ from brand name drugs, and what is done to ensure their safety and effectiveness. 3 pp. 601K. Free.

EXERCISE & DIET

FITNESS AND EXERCISE
Get fit and feel better with daily activities that fit the weather, your lifestyle, and your schedule. 12 pp. 605K. Free.

LOSING WEIGHT: MORE THAN COUNTING CALORIES
Use this guide to learn whether you're overweight, develop healthier eating habits, increase your physical activity, and create a successful weight loss plan. 6 pp. 523K. Free.

QUESTIONS & ANSWERS ABOUT ARTHRITIS AND EXERCISE
Suggestions on the best exercises to include in a program to help treat arthritis. 18 pp. 529K. Free.

WALKING FOR EXERCISE AND PLEASURE
Illustrated warm-up exercises and advice on how far, how fast, and how often for the best results. 14 pp. 122K. $1.25.

WEIGHT LOSS: FINDING A WEIGHT LOSS PROGRAM THAT WORKS FOR YOU
Tips on comparing different weight loss programs and using the Body Mass Index (BMI) calculator to determine your BMI and set your weight goal. 11 pp. 325K. 50¢.

MEDICAL PROBLEMS

ANXIETY-FACT SHEET
Describes different types of anxiety disorders and what you can do if you recognize these symptoms in yourself or a loved one. 4 pp. 556K. Free.

ARTHRITIS AND RHEUMATIC DISEASES
Basic facts about these conditions, including examples of rheumatic diseases, symptoms, causes, diagnosis, and treatments. 34 pp. 555K. Free.

ATOPIC DERMATITIS
Find out more about the symptoms and treatments for this disease, which causes extremely itchy, inflamed skin. 37 pp. 558K. Free.

BONING UP ON OSTEOPOROSIS
You can lose bone mass over many years without warning. Learn the risk factors, diagnosis, and treatment options for preventing, minimizing, and even building back bone mass. 7 pp. 534K. Free.

CATARACT IN ADULTS
Cataract is a normal part of aging vision, but if it makes routine tasks too difficult, you may need surgery. Learn more about symptoms and treatments. 13 pp. 123K. $1.00.

CONTROLLING ASTHMA
Discusses what triggers an asthma attack, possible causes, and medications to prevent attacks and help relieve symptoms. 5 pp. 551K. Free.

DIABETES
One-third of the people who have diabetes in the U.S. are unaware they have the disease. Learn more about diabetes, its risk factors, warning signs, and treatments available. 6 pp. 564K. Free.

DO I HAVE ARTHRITIS?
Read about common signs of arthritis and how medications and exercise can help. 28 pp. 561K. Free.

EATING DISORDERS
Learn the symptoms of different eating diseases, who is most likely to be affected, and various treatment options. 8 pp. 521K. Free.

JUVENILE RHEUMATOID ARTHRITIS
This disease affects children 16 years old and younger. Find out about the causes, symptoms, tests, and various treatments. 19 pp. 502K. Free.

LUPUS
Lupus is a disease in which the immune system attacks the body's healthy cells and tissues. Discover more about lupus, including warning signs and available treatments. 33 pp. 563K. Free.

OSTEOARTHRITIS
Learn about symptoms, treatments, and helpful exercises for the most common type of arthritis. 36 pp. 562K. Free.

PREVENTING STROKE
Learn more about the most common cause of adult-disability and estimate your risk with the stroke-risk chart. 8 pp. 329K. 50¢.

PROSTATE CANCER: NO ONE ANSWER FOR TESTING OR TREATMENT
How prostate cancer is detected, what the stages are, and what you need to know to choose the best treatment option. 6 pp. 524K. Free.

QUESTIONS & ANSWERS ABOUT ACNE
Different types need different treaments and medications. Learn how acne develops, what treatments will and won't work, and how to care for your skin. 12 pp. 508K. Free.

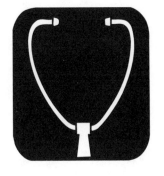

QUESTIONS & ANSWERS ABOUT ARTHRITIS PAIN
Get the facts on available options (conventional and

alternative) for short-term relief and long-term pain management. 18 pp. 530K. Free.

QUESTIONS & ANSWERS ABOUT GOUT
Here are details on this painful type of arthritis, its symptoms and treatments, and more. 11 pp. 531K. Free.

QUESTIONS & ANSWERS ABOUT HIP REPLACEMENT
Who is a likely candidate, alternatives available, possible complications, and what to expect during recovery and rehabilitation. 15 pp. 533K. Free.

QUESTIONS & ANSWERS ABOUT KNEE PROBLEMS
Causes, symptoms, diagnosis, and treatment of specific knee conditions. 30 pp. 535K. Free.

QUESTIONS & ANSWERS ABOUT ROSACEA
Learn about the possible causes, treatments available, and how to minimize flare-ups. 10 pp. 532K. Free.

REACTIVE ARTHRITIS
This form of arthritis occurs as a reaction to an infection in other parts of the body. Learn more about this condition, causes, symptoms, diagnosis, treatments available, and more. 17 pp. 606K. Free.

RHEUMATOID ARTHRITIS
Discusses diagnosis and treatment, with a medication chart for drug benefits and side effects. 33 pp. 566K. Free.

SO YOU HAVE HIGH BLOOD CHOLESTEROL
Here are the facts about high cholesterol and what you can do to lower yours. 36 pp. 124K. $1.75.

UNDERSTANDING TREATMENT CHOICES FOR PROSTATE CANCER
Prostate cancer patients face many treatment choices. Find out how prostate cancer is diagnosed, available treatment options, and follow-up care. 44 pp. 554K. Free.

URINARY TRACT INFECTIONS IN ADULTS
Find out more about the causes, symptoms, and treatments available. 8 pp. 330K. 50¢.

FOOD

ARE BIOENGINEERED FOODS SAFE?
Get the facts on what bioengineering is, how it affects humans, and what the FDA is doing to regulate the industry. 6 pp. 538K. Free.

COOKING FOR GROUPS: A VOLUNTEER'S GUIDE TO FOOD SAFETY
Whether it's a family reunion buffet or community cookout, learn how to cook and serve food safely and avoid food-borne illness. 40 pp. 539K. Free.

DIABETES RECIPES
Five tasty and easy-to-follow recipes for people with diabetes. Nutrition facts for each dish help you keep track of what you are eating. 5 pp. 565K. Free.

EAT RIGHT TO HELP LOWER YOUR HIGH BLOOD PRESSURE
Lists menu ideas and recipes to help you control your weight and high blood pressure. 30 pp. 116K. $4.25.

FIGHT BAC(TM): FOUR SIMPLE STEPS TO FOOD SAFETY
Advice on how to handle food safely so you, your family, and friends don't become ill. 5 pp. 552K. Free.

FOOD ALLERGIES: WHEN FOOD BECOMES THE ENEMY
Find out more about food allergies, what causes them, how to manage them, and more. 6 pp. 522K. Free.

FOOD GUIDE PYRAMID
Use this guide to select the nutrients you need and reduce the fat, cholesterol, and sodium in your diet. 29 pp. 118K. $1.00.

GET ON THE GRAIN TRAIN
Get the facts on the important role grain plays in your diet-its benefits, different types, how many servings you need, what counts as a serving, and more. 4 pp. 125K. $2.00.

GROWING OLDER, EATING BETTER
Discusses the various causes of poor nutrition and how it can be improved. 5 pp. 537K. Free.

How Much Are You Eating?

Learn how much you need each day from each of the five food groups and how to compare what you eat with what is recommended so that you don't overeat. 6 pp. 115K. $2.25.

Listeriosis and Food Safety Tips

Eating foods with the listeria bacteria can seriously affect pregnant women, newborns, and older adults. Learn about this illness, its symptoms, and prevention tips. 8 pp. 553K. Free.

Recipes and Tips for Healthy, Thrifty Meals

How to create healthy and budget-friendly meals-with tips on planning meals, shopping lists, a sample 2-week menu, and 40 great recipes. 76 pp. 119K. $5.50.

Thermy(tm): Use a Food Thermometer

Get the right thermometer and use this handy temperature chart for safe, delicious food. 4 pp. 541K. Free.

To Your Health! Food Safety for Seniors

Covers the basic rules of safe food preparation, including a list of foods not recommended for those over 65. 17 pp. 540K. Free.

Using the Dietary Guidelines for Americans

How to choose a diet that will taste good, be nutritious, and reduce chronic disease risks. 8 pp. 321K. 50¢.

CARS

Buying a New Car

Here's a step-by-step guide that is a helpful tool for bargaining with dealers. 2 pp. 301K. 50¢.

Buying a Used Car

Discusses your limited rights when buying from a dealer or private owner. 16 pp. 302K. 50¢.

Finding the Best Used Car

Covers what to look for on the test drive, warning signs of hidden damage, and how to verify the car's history. 10 pp. 509K. Free.

GLOVE BOX TIPS
Six booklets to help you get your car ready for summer and winter driving, choose the right repair shop, and get the best work from your mechanic. 19 pp. 368K. $1.00.

HOW TO FIND YOUR WAY UNDER THE HOOD & AROUND THE CAR
Instructions for 14 preventive maintenance services you can perform on your car. 2 pp. 308K. 50¢.

HOW TO GET A GREAT DEAL ON A NEW CAR
Step-by-step details for a proven negotiation technique to save money on your next car. 4 pp. 305K. 50¢.

NINE WAYS TO LOWER YOUR AUTO INSURANCE COSTS
Tips on how to reduce your expenses. Includes a chart to compare discounts. 2 pp. 307K. 50¢.

TAKING THE SCARE OUT OF AUTO REPAIR
Keep your car running smoothly with these practical tips on spotting trouble, choosing a repair shop, and working with your mechanic. 15 pp. 306K. 50¢.

COMPUTERS

DOT CONS
Find out about the top ten online scams, how you can protect yourself, and tips for surfing the Internet without getting swindled. 3 pp. 312K. 50¢.

INTERNET AUCTIONS: A GUIDE FOR BUYERS AND SELLERS
Learn more about how Internet auctions work, payment options, and how to protect yourself. 18 pp. 359K. 50¢.

SHOP SAFELY ONLINE
Is it really safe? Here are the facts about buying over the Internet and how to protect yourself. 2 pp. 361K. 50¢.

SITE-SEEING ON THE INTERNET
How to the navigate the Internet, learn the local customs and lingo, and know what to avoid during your travels. 11 pp. 362K. 50¢.

Yᴏᴜ'ᴠᴇ Gᴏᴛ Sᴘᴀᴍ: Hᴏᴡ ᴛᴏ "Cᴀɴ" Uɴᴡᴀɴᴛᴇᴅ E-ᴍᴀɪʟ
Find out how marketers get your e-mail address, how to reduce the amount of spam you receive, what to do with it, and more. 2 pp. 322K. 50¢.

EDUCATION

Eᴅᴜᴄᴀᴛɪᴏɴᴀʟ Pᴏsᴛᴇʀ ᴏɴ Wᴀᴛᴇʀ Pᴏʟʟᴜᴛɪᴏɴ
Learn where our drinking water comes from, potential threats to the safety of our water, and what is being done to protect it. Poster. 590K. Free.

Fɪɴᴀɴᴄɪᴀʟ Pʟᴀɴɴɪɴɢ ғᴏʀ Cᴏʟʟᴇɢᴇ
Strategies to help you plan for tuition and fees, along with helpful charts for estimating future costs. 10 pp. 510K. Free.

GED Iɴғᴏʀᴍᴀᴛɪᴏɴ Bᴜʟʟᴇᴛɪɴ
The revised Bulletin explains the content of the new GED Tests, how to prepare for the Tests, and how to get more information. 16 pp. 604K. Free.

Nᴏɴᴛʀᴀᴅɪᴛɪᴏɴᴀʟ Eᴅᴜᴄᴀᴛɪᴏɴ: Aʟᴛᴇʀɴᴀᴛɪᴠᴇ Wᴀʏs ᴛᴏ Eᴀʀɴ Yᴏᴜʀ Cʀᴇᴅᴇɴᴛɪᴀʟs
Get high school or college credit through the GED program, the National External Diploma program, correspondence and distance study, and standardized tests. 13 pp. 101K. $2.75.

EMPLOYMENT

Aᴘᴘʀᴇɴᴛɪᴄᴇsʜɪᴘs: Cᴀʀᴇᴇʀ Tʀᴀɪɴɪɴɢ, Cʀᴇᴅᴇɴᴛɪᴀʟs- ᴀɴᴅ ᴀ Pᴀʏᴄʜᴇᴄᴋ ɪɴ Yᴏᴜʀ Pᴏᴄᴋᴇᴛ
Apprenticeships are available in more than 850 occupations. Learn how these programs work and how to choose the best program for you. 20 pp. 102K. $3.50.

Eᴍᴘʟᴏʏᴍᴇɴᴛ Iɴᴛᴇʀᴠɪᴇᴡɪɴɢ
Gives useful advice on what to do before, during, and after a job interview. Includes tips about job fairs. 9 pp. 103K. $1.75.

Hᴇʟᴘ Wᴀɴᴛᴇᴅ-Fɪɴᴅɪɴɢ ᴀ Jᴏʙ
Describes both private companies and government agencies that offer help in finding a job. Lists precautions to take when contacting an employment service firm. 1 pp. 316K. 50¢.

HIGH EARNING WORKERS WHO DON'T HAVE A BACHELOR'S DEGREE
Identifies 50 occupations requiring less than a bachelor's degree. 9 pp. 105K. $3.25.

PENSION AND HEALTH CARE COVERAGE... QUESTIONS & ANSWERS FOR DISLOCATED WORKERS
Explains what happens to your health and pension benefits if you lose your job or your hours are reduced below full-time. 32 pp. 589K. Free.

RESUMES, APPLICATIONS, AND COVER LETTERS
Use this guide's samples to prepare a winning cover letter and resume. 15 pp. 108K. $2.00.

TIPS FOR FINDING THE RIGHT JOB
Assess your skills and interests, create a resume, write cover letters, and prepare for a job interview. 27 pp. 109K. $2.50.

TOP 10 WAYS TO MAKE YOUR HEALTH BENEFITS WORK FOR YOU
It's easy to become overwhelmed with choosing, filing for, and understanding health benefits. Use these 10 easy tips to get the most out of your health benefit options. 2 pp. 525K. Free.

FAMILY

BLACK FAMILY RESEARCH: RECORDS OF POST-CIVIL WAR FEDERAL AGENCIES AT THE NATIONAL ARCHIVES
Learn how to access information on marriages, births, deaths, occupations, places of residence, and other family-related matters in the post-Civil War era. 23 pp. 107K. $2.25.

CATCH THE SPIRIT: A STUDENT'S GUIDE TO COMMUNITY SERVICE
Ideas and information on how young people can help make their community a better place. 15 pp. 501K. Free.

FUN PLAY, SAFE PLAY
Discover the importance of play in your child's learning and development. Suggests toys for different ages. 18 pp. 503K. Free.

GOT A SICK KID? THE RIGHT MEDICATION, IN THE RIGHT DOSAGE, CAN BE CRITICAL
Follow these tips whenever giving medication, and use the recommended vaccine schedule to protect against 12 major childhood diseases. 3 pp. 507K. Free.

HANDBOOK ON CHILD SUPPORT ENFORCEMENT
A "how to" guide for getting the payments owed to you and your children. Lists state and federal offices to contact for more information. 61 pp. 505K. Free.

KIDS AND THEIR BONES: A PARENTS' GUIDE
Taking care of your child's bones now can protect against later fractures and possible osteoporosis. Learn about the factors that may affect the health of your child's bones. 11 pp. 504K. Free.

MY HISTORY IS AMERICA'S HISTORY
This 17" x 22" poster has easy ideas for discovering and preserving your family's history, with useful tips on recording family stories. 360K. 50¢.

YOUR FAMILY DISASTER SUPPLIES KIT
Lists kinds of food, first aid supplies, tools, and other items you should stock for an emergency. 4 pp. 364K. 50¢.

FEDERAL PROGRAMS

AMERICANS WITH DISABILITIES ACT: QUESTIONS AND ANSWERS
Explains how the civil rights of persons with disabilities are protected at work and in public places. 31 pp. 513K. Free.

ARE THERE ANY PUBLIC LANDS FOR SALE?
Describes the federal program to sell excess undeveloped public land and why there is no more available for homesteading. 12 pp. 111K. $1.50.

A GUIDE TO DISABILITY RIGHTS LAWS
Covers the rights of persons with disabilities regarding fair housing, public accommodations, telecommunications, education, and employment. 14 pp. 514K. Free.

GUIDE TO FEDERAL GOVERNMENT SALES
Explains how to buy homes, cars, and other property from 20 federal sales programs. 21 pp. 112K. $2.00.

HOW YOU CAN BUY USED FEDERAL PERSONAL PROPERTY
Describes used equipment and industrial items sold by the government, how they are sold, and where to call for more information. 5 pp. 318K. 50¢.

NATIONAL SELLERS LIST
List of addresses and phone numbers for dealers who sell real estate and personal property that have been forfeited to federal law enforcement agencies. 8 pp. 319K. 50¢.

SOCIAL SECURITY: YOUR NUMBER AND CARD
Explains why we have social security numbers, when and how to get one, and how to protect your privacy. 2 pp. 515K. Free.

U.S. REAL PROPERTY SALES LIST
Learn about government real estate properties that are sold by auction or sealed bid and how to get more information on specific properties. 5 pp. 559K. Free.

YOUR RIGHT TO FEDERAL RECORDS
Use the Freedom of Information Act (FOIA) and the Privacy Act to obtain records from the federal government. Includes sample request letters. 33 pp. 320K. 50¢.

BENEFITS

FEDERAL BENEFITS FOR VETERANS AND DEPENDENTS
Explains disability, pension, health care, education and housing loans, and other benefit programs for veterans and their families. 114 pp. 113K. $5.00.

REQUEST FOR SOCIAL SECURITY STATEMENT
Complete this form and return it to Social Security to get your earnings history and an estimate of future benefits. 3 pp. 516K. Free.

SOCIAL SECURITY: BASIC FACTS
Describes the different kinds of Social Security ben-

efits, who receives them, and how they're financed. 17 pp. 517K. Free.

SOCIAL SECURITY: UNDERSTANDING THE BENEFITS
Explains retirement, disability, survivor's benefits, Medicare coverage, Supplemental Security Income, and more. 39 pp. 518K. Free.

SOCIAL SECURITY: WHAT EVERY WOMAN SHOULD KNOW
Discusses how a woman's benefits may be affected by disability, divorce, widowhood, retirement, or other special situations. 19 pp. 519K. Free.

HOUSING
FINANCING & SALES

BORROWER'S GUIDE TO HOME LOANS
How to find the best loan for your needs when shopping for home equity loans and reverse mortgages. 16 pp. 595K. Free.

FINANCING AN ENERGY-EFFICIENT HOME
Find mortgages and home improvement loans to make your home more energy efficient. 8 pp. 131K. $2.00.

GUIDE TO SINGLE-FAMILY HOME MORTGAGE INSURANCE
Explains FHA mortgage insurance programs, including types available, how to qualify, how to apply, restrictions, and more. 14 pp. 332K. 50¢.

HIGH-COST "PREDATORY" HOME LOANS: HOW TO AVOID THE TRAPS
You can protect yourself by knowing the warning signs of predatory loan practices, questions to ask before signing a contract, and where to turn for help. 12 pp. 596K. Free.

HOW TO BUY A HOME WITH A LOW DOWN PAYMENT
Describes how to qualify for a low down payment mortgage, determine what you can afford, and how mortgage insurance works. 9 pp. 570K. Free.

HOW TO BUY A MANUFACTURED (MOBILE) HOME
Tips on selection and placement, warranties, site

preparation, transportation, installation, and more. 14 pp. 333K. 50¢.

HUD Home Buying Guide
Step-by-step instructions for finding and financing a HUD home. Includes charts to help you estimate mortgage payments. 11 pp. 571K. Free.

Looking for the Best Mortgage-Shop, Compare, Negotiate
Use these 3 steps to save money on a mortgage or home loan. Includes a mortgage shopping worksheet. 7 pp. 334K. 50¢.

Twelve Ways to Lower Your Homeowners Insurance Costs
Includes tips on saving money, with phone numbers of state insurance departments for more information. 4 pp. 335K. 50¢.

Home Maintenance

Am I Covered?
Answers 15 common questions regarding homeowners insurance and explains what is covered in a standard policy. 9 pp. 336K. 50¢.

Cooling Your Home Naturally
Ways to save electricity and keep your home cool with landscaping, roof treatments, shading, windows, and more. 8 pp. 126K. $2.00.

Energy Savers: Tips on Saving Energy & Money at Home
Reduce your home energy use with tips on insulation, weatherization, heating, and more. 36 pp. 337K. 50¢.

Energy-Efficient Air Conditioning
Explains how air conditioners work, what different types are available, and how to troubleshoot and maintain your air conditioners. 8 pp. 128K. $1.50.

Healthy Lawn, Healthy Environment
Tips on lawn care, including soil preparation, watering, mowing, pesticides, and choosing a lawn care service. 19 pp. 338K. 50¢.

Home Sweet Home Improvement
Warning signs of a shady contractor, questions to

ask to protect yourself from fraud, and tips on re-
solving complaints. 12 pp. 304K. 50¢.

HOW TO PRUNE TREES
Illustrated guide shows what to do, what not to do,
tools to use and when to produce healthy, strong
trees. 30 pp. 129K. $2.00.

INDOOR AIR HAZARDS EVERY HOMEOWNER SHOULD KNOW ABOUT
How to get rid of molds, carbon monoxide, radon,
asbestos, lead, tobacco smoke, and other pollutants.
16 pp. 549K. Free.

NATIONAL FLOOD INSURANCE GUIDE
Property owners can purchase insurance against
flooding losses. Learn the requirements, questions
to ask, and more. 20 pp. 597K. Free.

POWER$MART: EASY TIPS TO SAVE MONEY AND THE PLANET
Tips on making your home more comfortable while
reducing your monthly energy bill. 24 pp. 573K.
Free.

SELECTING A NEW WATER HEATER
Describes how different types of water heaters work
and important features to consider when buying. 6
pp. 130K. $1.25.

SURGES HAPPEN!
How to Protect the Appliances in Your Home. Find
out what power surges are, what appliances need
protection, and what devices work best. 20 pp. 104K.
$2.25.

MONEY

ESTABLISHING A TRUST FUND
Learn what different kinds of trusts can and can't
do, their benefits, the role of a trustee, and more. 10
pp. 574K. Free.

LIVING TRUST OFFERS
Find out if living trusts are right for you and how
to protect yourself from scams when planning your
estate. 2 pp. 365K. 50¢.

MAKING A WILL
Explains why a will is important, how to prepare

one, what to include, and how to keep it current. 12 pp. 575K. Free.

PLANNING YOUR ESTATE
How to estimate the size of your estate, minimize taxes, and provide for your heirs. 10 pp. 577K. Free.

PRIVACY CHOICES FOR YOUR PERSONAL FINANCIAL INFORMATION
Explains your right to opt out of sharing some of your personal information and lists the types of information that financial companies can share about you. 8 pp. 309K. 50¢.

WHEN IS YOUR CHECK NOT A CHECK?
Learn about your rights when it comes to electronic check conversion and what to do if you have a problem. 2 pp. 339K. 50¢.

CREDIT

BUILDING A BETTER CREDIT RECORD
Learn how to legally improve your credit report, deal with debt, spot credit-related scams, and more. 16 pp. 303K. 50¢.

CONSUMER HANDBOOK TO CREDIT PROTECTION LAWS
Consumer credit laws explain what you should look for when using credit, details that creditors look for before extending credit, and more. 44 pp. 340K. 50¢.

CREDIT MATTERS
How to qualify for credit, keep a good credit history, protect your credit, and more. 2 pp. 341K. 50¢.

FAIR CREDIT REPORTING
Learn what's in your credit report, how you can get a copy, and more. 2 pp. 342K. 50¢.

HOW TO DISPUTE CREDIT REPORT ERRORS
Gives tips on correcting errors, registering a dispute, and adding information to your file. 2 pp. 344K. 50¢.

IDENTITY THEFT: REDUCE YOUR RISK
How to protect your personal information, what to do if you are a victim, resources to contact, and more. 7 pp. 623K. Free.

INVESTING & SAVING

66 WAYS TO SAVE MONEY
Practical ways to cut everyday costs on transportation, insurance, banking, credit, housing, utilities, food, and more. 4 pp. 347K. 50¢.

BUILD WEALTH NOT DEBT
Join the American Saver program-learn 5 key savings strategies and receive a free quarterly savings newsletter. 6 pp. 594K. Free.

BUILDING FINANCIAL FREEDOM
Features a worksheet to help track your spending, tips on creating a financial plan, and an investor's checklist. 12 pp. 579K. Free.

CERTIFICATES OF DEPOSIT: TIPS FOR INVESTORS
Learn how CDs work, how to purchase them, and questions to ask before buying. 2 pp. 350K. 50¢.

THE CONSUMER'S ALMANAC
Organize your bills, save and invest for the future, and manage your debt with monthly calendars and worksheets. 32 pp. 348K. 50¢.

GET THE FACTS ON SAVING AND INVESTING
Use this guide's helpful tips and worksheets to calculate income, expenses, and net worth. 18 pp. 349K. 50¢.

HOW SIPC PROTECTS YOU
If your brokerage firm closes due to bankruptcy or other financial difficulties, the Securities Investor Protection Corporation works to return your assets. Find out what SIPC does and does not cover. 10 pp. 543K. Free.

HOW TO CHECK OUT YOUR STOCKBROKER OR BROKERAGE FIRM/WHEN YOUR BROKER CALLS, TAKE NOTES!
Request a Central Registration Depository report to get your stockbroker's history and background. Use the worksheet to make notes and keep track of recommendations. 5 pp. 599K. Free.

INVESTORS' BILL OF RIGHTS
What you should know about investments and what information you are entitled to before investing. 7 pp. 578K. Free.

TEN QUESTIONS TO ASK WHEN CHOOSING A FINANCIAL PLANNER
An interview checklist covers credentials, costs, and services. Also includes resources to contact for more information. 12 pp. 580K. Free.

U.S. SAVINGS BONDS
Learn about the different types of bonds, federal and state tax benefits, and how to purchase bonds online. 7 pp. 346K. 50¢.

WHAT YOU SHOULD KNOW ABOUT FINANCIAL PLANNING
Discusses the benefits of financial planning for life-changing events, such as buying a home or retirement. 13 pp. 581K. Free.

YOUR INSURED DEPOSIT
Explains what is protected and what isn't if your bank should fail, how much of your money is insured, what types of accounts are covered, and more. 21 pp. 582K. Free.

YOUR RIGHTS AS A FINANCIAL PLANNING CLIENT
Know your rights, what to expect from your financial planner, and what to do if you have a problem. 5 pp. 572K. Free.

RETIREMENT PLANNING

401(K) PLANS
Explains what these plans are, what happens when you change employers, and what to do if you need the money before retirement. 14 pp. 583K. Free.

ANNUITIES
Learn about the different types of annuities and take a helpful quiz to see if they are right for you. 11 pp. 584K. Free.

SAVINGS FITNESS: A GUIDE TO YOUR MONEY AND YOUR FINANCIAL FUTURE
Create your personal savings plan and prepare for retirement with this step-by-step guide. 20 pp. 585K. Free.

TOP 10 WAYS TO PREPARE FOR RETIREMENT
Gives practical tips to build your retirement sav-

ings and lists resources for more information. 2 pp. 586K. Free.

VARIABLE ANNUITIES: WHAT YOU SHOULD KNOW
Explains what they are, how they work, what you have to pay, and questions to ask before you invest. 20 pp. 366K. 50¢.

WOMEN AND RETIREMENT SAVINGS
What women need to know about retirement benefits, including plan type, eligibility, penalties, spousal benefits, and more. 6 pp. 587K. Free.

YOUR GUARANTEED PENSION
Answers 18 frequently-asked questions about the security of private pension plans, including benefits and plan termination. 12 pp. 588K. Free.

SMALL BUSINESS

ADVANCE FEE BUSINESS SCAMS
Find out about the different types of advance fee scams, how to spot them, and what you should do if you're a victim. 5 pp. 351K. 50¢.

A CONSUMER GUIDE TO BUYING A FRANCHISE
Learn about the benefits of franchise ownership, the limitations, choosing the best franchise for you, and more. 18 pp. 311K. 50¢.

COPYRIGHT BASICS
Covers what can be copyrighted, who can apply, registration procedures, filing fees, what forms to use, and more. 12 pp. 354K. 50¢.

FACTS ABOUT...STARTING A SMALL BUSINESS
How to create a business plan, research your market, raise money for your business, and more. 16 pp. 353K. 50¢.

GUIDE TO BUSINESS CREDIT FOR WOMEN, MINORITIES, AND SMALL BUSINESSES
Know what loans are available, the credit approval process, and your legal rights. 12 pp. 317K. 50¢.

INTRODUCTION TO FEDERAL TAXES FOR SMALL BUSINESS/SELF-EMPLOYED
This helpful CD-ROM walks you through the tax year and explains how to document expenses and deductions and file federal taxes. 369K. $1.00.

SBA Programs & Services
Learn about the U.S. Small Business Administration's financial assistance and business development programs to help you start or expand a business. 40 pp. 607K. Free.

Virtual Small Business Workshop
This user-friendly CD-ROM covers a variety of small business tax issues, including payroll taxes, electronic filing, and recordkeeping. 370K. $1.00.

TRAVEL

Fly Smart
Gives more than 30 steps you can take to help make your flight a safe one. 2 pp. 560K. Free.

Fly-Rights
Helpful advice for travelers on getting the best fares, what to do with lost tickets and baggage, canceled flights, and more. 58 pp. 134K. $4.00.

Foreign Entry Requirements
Lists 200 embassy and consulate addresses and phone numbers where visas may be obtained. 21 pp. 326K. 50¢.

Lesser Known Areas of the National Park System
Listing by state of more than 170 national parks, their accommodations, locations, and historical significance. 49 pp. 135K. $3.00.

National Park System Map and Guide
Full-color map lists activities at more than 300 parks, monuments, and historic sites. 136K. $1.25.

National Trails System Map and Guide
Full-color map describes eight national scenic trails and nine national historic trails. 137K. $1.25.

National Wildlife Refuges: A Visitor's Guide
Use this full-color map to plan a visit and learn about hundreds of endangered species and their habitats. 138K. $1.75.

Passports: Applying for Them the Easy Way
How, when, and where to apply for U.S. passports.

Includes information on fees. 12 pp. 355K. 50¢.

SAFE TRIP ABROAD
How to take precautions against robbery, terrorism, or other dangers. What to do if you find yourself in trouble while abroad. 20 pp. 140K. $2.50.

TIPS FOR WOMEN TRAVELING ALONE
Traveling on your own can be an adventure-make sure it's a safe one with these helpful tips. 5 pp. 327K. 50¢.

TRAVEL SMART: TRAVEL SAFE
Tips on getting health and safety warnings, passport and visa requirements, and more when visiting other countries. 6 pp. 356K. 50¢.

TRAVEL TIPS FOR STUDENTS
Trips abroad can be an exciting part of your education-use these tips to make sure your trip is trouble-free and safe. 5 pp. 328K. 50¢.

WASHINGTON: THE NATION'S CAPITAL
Use this guide to learn more about our country's heritage by exploring Washington D.C. 139K. $1.25.

AND MORE...

2003 CONSUMER ACTION HANDBOOK
Get help with consumer problems and complaints. Find consumer contacts at hundreds of companies and trade associations, local, state, and federal government agencies, national consumer organizations, and more. 172 pp. 568K. Free.

AMERICAN REVOLUTION AT A GLANCE
Learn about the major battles with colorful maps and informative descriptions. 114K. $2.00.

CIVIL WAR AT A GLANCE
This full-color map illustrates and briefly describes major Civil War battle campaigns. 121K. $2.00.

CONSERVING AMERICA'S FISHERIES
Did you know that more than 100 kinds of American fish are endangered? Find out what is being done to restore our fisheries and how you can help. 7 pp. 592K. Free.

CONSERVING THE NATURE OF AMERICA
Beautiful photos show how fish, wildlife, and plants

are protected in more than 500 National Wildlife Refuges. Also gives details on volunteer and recreational opportunities. 24 pp. 591K. Free.

CONSTITUTION OF THE UNITED STATES AND THE DECLARATION OF INDEPENDENCE
Learn more about the foundations of our country's freedom with these historic documents. 48 pp. 110K. $2.50.

FISHING IS FUN FOR EVERYONE
Find out what equipment you'll need, what kind of bait to use, how to cast and tie knots, and where to fish for more information. 11 pp. 593K. Free.

FOR THE BIRDS
How to attract different species of birds, feed them, and select suitable homes. 50 pp. 357K. 50¢.

FUNERALS: A CONSUMER GUIDE
Know your rights as a consumer and what to keep in mind when making funeral arrangements. 30 pp. 358K. 50¢.

GETTYSBURG NATIONAL MILITARY PARK
It's the site of one of the most important battles in the American Civil War. Learn more with maps, photographs, and a day-to-day history of the key battle that took place there. 64 pp. 117K. $5.00.

GOING WIRELESS: A CONSUMER GUIDE TO CHOOSING CELLULAR SERVICE
How to select the right phone and calling plan, understand the terms of your contract, avoid fraud, and more. 8 pp. 603K. Free.

LISTA DE PUBLICACIONES FEDERALES EN ESPA—OL PARA EL CONSUMIDOR
Lists 200 free publications in Spanish available from federal agencies. Bulk copies of this publication are available. 16 pp. 567K. Free.

OUR FLAG
Are you familiar with the U.S. flag's history and customs? Here is everything you want to know about the flag. 52 pp. 120K. $3.25.

U.S. AND THE METRIC SYSTEM
Explains how to use metric in everyday life. Includes

metric conversion charts and more. 10 pp. 363K. 50¢.

WHERE TO WRITE FOR VITAL RECORDS
This useful guide offers listings by state on obtaining birth, death, marriage, and divorce certificates. 47 pp. 132K. $3.25.

ONLINE ONLY

These best-sellers are no longer available in print from FCIC but their full text can be viewed on our website. Just visit: **www.pueblo.gsa.gov/online.htm**

KEEPING FAMILY/HOUSEHOLD RECORDS
Organize your bills, tax information, legal papers and other important documents. Learn what to keep and how to safeguard your important documents.

A CONSUMER'S GUIDE TO FATS
Learn about the different kinds and what effect they have on your cholesterol level.

FDA GUIDE TO DIETARY SUPPLEMENTS
This informative guide can help you make educated decisions regarding these products and determine if their claims, such as improving memory or energy, are true.

THE STUDENT GUIDE TO FINANCIAL AID
This valuable resource explains grants, loans, work-study programs, and how to apply for them.

FIXING UP YOUR HOME AND HOW TO FINANCE IT
Information about hiring a contractor, doing the work yourself, and the HUD Title 1 home improvement loan program.

MEDICARE AND HOME HEALTH CARE
Outlines the home health care benefit, who is eligible, how to find an approved home health agency, and more.

FRUITS AND VEGETABLES: EATING YOUR WAY TO 5 A DAY
Eating fruits and vegetables can reduce the risk of heart disease and cancer. Gives ideas to help you meet the 5 A Day goal.

ORDERING INFORMATION

You'll notice that some booklets have a price and others are entirely free. The small price that may be charged helps the government pay a part of the cost to print and distribute these useful booklets.

However, all of these booklets can be viewed, downloaded and printed by going to the following web site:

www.pueblo.gsa.gov

HOW TO ORDER

Select the publications you would like to order. At the end of each listing there is a item number followed by either a price or the word 'Free' (for example, the **'Travel Tips for Students'** booklet has the item number and price .... 328K. 50¢. Write down the item number and include a check, money order or charge card information (including expiration date and your signature) with your order and send it to:

FCIC - 03B
PO Box 100
Pueblo, CO 81002

While there is no charge for individual free publications, there is a $2.00 service fee to help defray program costs. For that $2.00, you may order up to 25 different free booklets. Payment can be made by check or money order made payable to the "Superintendent of Documents" or charged to your VISA, MasterCard or Discover card (include expiration date & signature.) Priority handling is available when orders placed by phone at an extra charge.

If you would like you can also order by phone using your credit card. Call: **1-888-878-3256**

Free Groceries & Gifts

- Recently a woman walked out of a Safeway super-market in Los Angeles with over $67 in groceries without paying for them. Shoplifting? No - it was all perfectly legal

- A woman in Brewster, N.Y. bought $80 in groceries. She paid 32 cents!

- A Yonkers, N.Y. woman bought over $130 worth of food and groceries. Her total cost was only $7.07.

- A New Jersey housewife purchased $32. worth of groceries. She handed over $3.00 to the cashier.

These women make it a habit to coupon their way to hundreds...even thousands...of dollars every year in free grocer-ies. These super-shoppers have learned to stretch the buying power of every dollar they spend.

They take advantage of the fact that many food and drug manu-facturers are anxious to pay you for trying their products. These companies offer you cash refunds, free product coupons, toys and gifts of all kinds.

Here are some tips that will help you save up to $2,000 every year on your grocery bill:

1. Buy only brand name items (not store brands or no-frills). It's only on brand name products that you will get the refund checks, coupons for free products and other free gifts offered by various manufacturers. For example, when Tide is offering Timex watches as a premium you buy Tide.

2. Look for supermarkets that double the value of coupons - many supermarkets will give you $1.00 off, for example, when you give them a 50 cents coupon.

3. Save parts of the packaging for future refunds and gifts. Com-panies will pay cash for certain parts of their packages (like boxtops and proof of purchase seals) as proof you purchased their products.

4. Carefully check supermarket circulars and newspaper ads for extra money- saving specials. Often you can combine these special sale prices with your coupons for a double- barrelled saving.

5. Quantity buying of specials. When your supermarket offers an extra special bargain buy more than you need right away. The more you buy the more you save.

6. Subscribe to a good refund magazine. A typical issue may contain between $100 and $200 in refund offers from hundreds of companies.

But coupons and refunds are just a part of the dollar stretcher system. A true super shopper is someone who refuses to pay more than they have to for anything they buy. But most people simply don't realize just how much their money can buy. For that reason we suggest you read the Dollar Stretcher Report.

Discover how to buy everything from film to furniture at 30% to 89% below retail. Learn how you can save hundreds of dollars on your utility bill, phone bill, car purchases, vacations. Make your savings earn the highest return and borrow money 30% -40% cheaper than the rate your bank charges.

If you'd like a copy of the Dollar Stretcher Report send $2.00 for S&H to:

DOLLAR STRETCHER REPORT
Box 125 - BFT
Hartsdale, NY 10530